THE ART OF PEACE

Raising Humanity

NICOLE MYERS HENDERSON

Foreword by C. Norm Shealy, M.D., PH.D.

SOUL PURPOSE

Information

Reprint Permission

Permission to reprint will be made available to responsible scholars upon request.

DISCLAIMERS

The information contained herein is for instructional and educational purposes only and should not be interpreted as medical or psychological counsel. Any information presented is related to medical remote viewing or cellular memory therapy is not intended to diagnose, treat, nor cure any health ailment nor act as a substitute for the advice of a licensed healthcare practitioner.

The materials compiled and shared for training in medical remote viewing and cellular memory therapy are not to be utilized to form a medical opinion or diagnosis without being supported by further testing and corroboration with licensed medical professionals. *These approaches are complementary adjuncts for clients wanting a second opinion from a psycho-spiritual point of view. Individuals are always encouraged to seek medical evaluations for their disorders, and this author always suggests medical confirmation of any suspected patho-physiology. In short, it is this author's suggestion that individuals take responsibility for their own health, thereby consulting a medical practitioner if one suspects the manifestation of a physical illness.*

Foreword

I have been the quintessential research scientist whose primary interest in life has been to discover the relationship between energy, the physical body and the sacred texture of the human being. Through an incredible breadth and depth of experience in the holistic and integrated medicine field, I remain passionate about human potential.

In 1956, I completed medical school and started my neurosurgical residency. I had assisted on a cordotomy, the most barbarian procedure in history—cutting the front half of the spinal cord with a razor blade! It made me determined to find other alternatives; anything as a safe alternative! It was then, it became evident that we must include spiritual, homeopathic, and 'safe exploration' of everything!

I was born to be a physician and scientist; venturing into full research mode after leaving neurosurgery to dive into the study of pain management. I went in search of alternative treatment for pain, interested in the realm of alternative methodologies for everything, including what's available from the psychic or spiritual realm. In pursuing research and alternative methodologies of healing, I found many that pushed through the barriers of even, alternative thinking. I experimented with ways to influence the delicate balance of the human energy system. Subtle body medicine has been my frontier and a vast space of opportunity for my mind to wonder while exploring human potential.

Throughout my career, I created the concept of Holistic Medicine in 1971 with the introduction of spinal cord stimulation and TENS and became editor of the Journal of Comprehensive Integrative Medicine. As founding president of the American Holistic Medical Association in 1978, my research led to the publishing of 36 books and over 350 articles on innovations including Electroacupuncture, Spinal Cord Stimulation, Transcutaneous Electrical Nerve Stimulation (TENS), the RejuvaMatrix ® for rejuvenating telomeres, and Transcutaneous Acupuncture, which also rejuvenates telomeres; Chakra Sweep Gamma PEMF for stress reduction and opioid addiction, Sapphire Enhanced Scalar for remarkable biochemical reduction in stress, and Biogenics Retraining of the Nervous System.

I am still active in clinical work, research, writing, education and remain a member of the Practical Pain Management Editorial Board. I say all of this to illuminate my praise of Nicole Myers Henderson's book *THE ART OF PEACE Raising Humanity*, her commitment, work ethic, heart and ongoing pursuit to ease suffering. She offers a grounded and practical approach to what is being shared. Her voice is valuable in that she speaks to the bridging of science and spirituality without leaning into the hokey, woo-woo or 'out-of-this -world' sensationalism. This is all-important in a world that is skeptical and guarded, while also in need of revolutionary solutions to health, healing and empowerment. We are a world that is on the precipice of profound change. Continual innocent entry into the scientific mind and the medical world remains essential. The research done in the past six decades has been a masterful contribution to the knowledge we need about our own bodies and capabilities.

In the Newtonian universe, the healing agents, drugs, doctors, surgery, hospitals — even healers and shamans — must be present in the same space and time as the patient, in order for healing to take place. It is unlikely we will ever be able to bypass physical means, like drugs and surgery for the healing of every disease in every person. A quantum universe is a set of probabilities susceptible to being influenced by many factors, including thought, will, and intention.

New insights clearly indicate that medicine isn't always the very first intervention point we should look to for physical and emotional healing. Research is screaming at us with the urgent message that consciousness can harness the powerful healing forces beyond a quantum universe. Our mind capacities are far more important and more potent than pills in a bottle.

It is becoming increasingly evident that the themes of the next millennium are healing, and the emergence of our sacred and soulful capacities into the entire web of life. This awareness points toward an awesome power over our own healing that is available from within. It returns the responsibility for our well-being to our own doorsteps, rather than displacing that responsibility onto some outside agent of healing.

In the emerging concept of the new sciences. There is no categorical divide between the physical world, the living world, and the world of mind and consciousness. Matter is vanishing as a fundamental feature of reality, retreating as basic elements of an energy-based universe.

The phenomenon, like healing across great distances, or even across time are conceivable. It is a universe in which spontaneous remission of disease is possible and in which the influence of a healer using non-physical means, can be as effective as conventional medical treatments.

Beyond the quantum universe, the energy field in which a patient exists can produce healing without any need for a spatial or temporal connection. The implications of such research are stunning. By changing our consciousness we can change the very blueprints around which our physical bodies are constructed. We can first seek healing close to the source by intervening in our own thinking, rather than trying to deal much later on down the line with the ill effects of our thoughts on our bodies. Whether you are a curious investigator or a beginner, this is a powerful first step toward your unlimited potential.

We typically think of psychics as special or gifted with unusual abilities. Anyone who has ever wondered if he or she could have the inherent skills shared within *THE ART OF PEACE,* will discover that each of us carries a dormant psychic ability we can explore and use ourselves. All human beings, including you, have an inborn capacity for the ability to see across space and time.

After 35 years, as a remote viewer, researcher and student of the quantum world, Nicole has created an accessible guide that introduces individuals to all of the essentials of remote viewing and cellular memory, while also providing a clear picture of the science behind the phenomena. This fascinating chronicle of life provides illustrations and answers. She presents comprehensive instruction for tapping into your ability to transcend the physical senses, by tapping into the collective, unconscious that connects everything in everyone in the universe.

Nicole has shared in a way that will speak to your mind and shift belief systems, while also connecting to your heart and soul confidence. Her goal is to initiate your capacity to access these inherent gifts of sight, hearing and oneness. This work will guide you, step by step, in discovering and controlling your own intuitive abilities even if you have been skeptical about having psychic abilities. This book shows you that you do because we all do. Through her own study and continual research, she has created a pathway to help you distinguish true, intuitive perceptions. She has compiled numerous experiences based on her work with clients in moving beyond limits that separate time, space and matter. *The Art of Peace* reveals how to use this information in practical ways in your own life.

Presented in an accessible, logical, and artful manner, here's an unprecedented training manual for learning this profoundly transformative practice, she offers hands-on beginner exercises as well as pointers. The mind has profound abilities, so much of which is still untapped by most. Healing, by definition, is a sacred art. It is a divine process in which healing the body first requires healing the spirit. Through this, the potential of technical and chemical medicine accelerates. For those interested in understanding the nature of healing, this book is a necessary part of any individual's library if they desire to take charge of not only healing themselves but also the world around them.

Nicole looks at the lessons of cell biology, quantum physics and brain physiology that shed light on the biophysical mechanisms at work in healing. *The Art of Peace* makes medical use of quantum coherence which gives rise to consciousness in order to affect healing, harnessing the healing power of consciousness. She urges our use of these superpowers in a pure-hearted, service-minded manner.

The Art of Peace, Raising Humanity is a broad subject, seemingly impossible for most people, yet completely possible for all! Hunches and gut feelings are just the tip of the iceberg in humanity's potential discoveries, ultimately leading us to an infinite well of creative expression and sacred oneness.

Through *The Art of Peace* Nicole is advocating for our super-human capacities and sovereignty within our own health and healing, but she also offers a glimpse into how this world can serve the unfolding of a whole new world. She presents an insightful view and experiential understanding of the seemingly impossible as possible; offering a view of what human beings could heal if their consciousness would only break free and breakthrough, of its illusions. Nicole Myers Henderson has created the 'encyclopedia of foundations of holism'. Imagine what our world might be like if all people could and would begin to hone their innate abilities afforded to them at birth.

C. NORMAN SHEALY, M.D., PH.D.

THE ART OF PEACE, Raising Humanity is dedicated to all sentient life here, now, and forever.

WE ARE ALL ONE. No matter how you try to maintain your individuality, you cannot be anything other than ONE piece of a much bigger puzzle that's connected to all life—all things. Everything you think and do affects all other life.

A message from the Editor

Henderson's THE ART OF PEACE, *Raising Humanity* is a text filled with unimaginable truths, shedding light on a reality I had been oblivious to my whole life. As a natural-born skeptic, I dove into Nicole's novel slightly closed off, but after just one chapter of page-flipping excitement, I was hooked, and I was immediately immersed in an entirely new world. With both anecdotes and scientific explanations, THE ART OF PEACE bridges the unfamiliar with the familiar, teaching us how to understand our bodies, read the signs they're giving us, and use that information to access parts of ourselves we didn't think we could access before. Struggling with multiple chronic illnesses that western medicine hasn't yet found a way to address, I've found refuge in the techniques presented, and since completing this book, have already learned how to hear my body when it speaks to me, and how to give it what it wants, tapping into my intuition and letting it guide me.

Contents

Introduction ~ Understanding Me

What and who I am at my core is a faithful servant of God, the Universal One, the creator and source of all things, who gifted this existence to me. The gifts or abilities I possess come with this body and it is my understanding that we all possess the same gifts. We just have to decide whether we want to develop them. I remember watching a movie as a child where a woman could feel what other people were feeling. By using her abilities, the woman began to perform healing acts for a church within her community. As if feeling the life of another wasn't enough, her body would emulate any dysfunction the sufferer was experiencing. At the end of the movie, it did not end so well for the healer. Her body took on the traits of all those who were suffering, and she was bedridden, completely frozen in a muscular contraction that would not allow her to move. I remember saying, "I want to be like her, but I won't let my body take on the sickness people feel." Imagine a young child being that aware, wanting to do something like this. There must have been some divine connection to past lives as a healer or maybe a deeper knowledge of choosing to enter this life to do such things.

The fact is, I purposefully chose to master my sensory skills. Why? I could feel the pain of people and animals, and it made me feel sad for them. It made me want to help, to seek solutions for their pains and sorrows. What they feel matters to me, and I was guided by some unseen force, down a long, arduous road academically and spiritually in an effort to pave the way for others like you to step into your own personal power, easily and effortlessly.

Some of my experiences were not pleasant. I often ran into people who doubted my abilities and I would spend countless hours beating myself up, wondering whether there was something wrong with me.

While living in east Florida in my twenties, a criminal case was brought to my attention. At the insistence of some unknown force, I called the police department to see if I could help. The lead detective told me he would have another detective visit me to go over the case. On the day we had scheduled to meet, I left my apartment door open for the detective to enter without knocking. I was standing in the kitchen when she walked up. She spoke in a slow, trembling voice.

"I am, um, looking for Nicole."

I said, "Sure, come on in and have a seat." She sat down at the kitchen table and pulled her briefcase to her lap. We spoke the normal niceties for a few minutes when I noticed her energy shift. As I felt her irritation, I asked her if I could be of some assistance to her case. She insisted she was there to see Nicole, but she felt like she had made a mistake. She felt like she was in the wrong place.

I felt her confusion and irritation, only I chose not to stop her as she got up and left suddenly. I left the door open. Fifteen minutes passed when she reappeared at the door. Without coming in she said, "I apologize. Am I in the right place? Does Nicole live here?"

"I am Nicole," I said.

She coughed as if choking at my words. "You can't be!"

"Why is that? Because I don't have beads hanging in my door, or because I'm not covered in gypsy garb? Or maybe I don't look old enough?"

"Actually, it's all the above."

I shrugged my shoulders and motioned for her to sit down at the table again.

"Please forgive me for saying this, but I'll need proof that you can do what I'm told you are capable of," she said with a painful grimace on her face.

"No apology necessary," I said. "I am getting accustomed to having to prove myself."

Proving that I was capable of seemingly extraordinary intuitive works got old, and after many years of being asked to jump through hoops, I decided that it was necessary to continue my education to be more believable. I would need to not only find a way to communicate more effectively, but I'd also have to educate myself on topics within specific fields of interest so that I could speak the language of the professionals with which I would ultimately work. I studied human anatomy, physiology, energy medicine, physics, integrative health, nutrition, business, law, metallurgy, horticulture, theology, animal husbandry, and environmental problem-solving, among others within many different academic forums. Then, through remote viewing, I learned that I didn't need to study all of those things. Not really. With remote viewing practices, if I were to know something about my target, it would naturally come up during the session. I learned a lot about myself in that my studies helped me feel more comfortable interacting within different fields and that when I focused my full attention and intention on a target or subject, I would stream information in from the multiverse and catch or extract the information I was meant to.

The things that challenged me to grow led me to move beyond paranormal belief ideologies. I'm thankful for that because knowing that there is a science behind intuition allows me to drop the fear, stop the taboo talk, and step into my power. I think that the scientific discoveries of yesterday left clues for us so that we could get here. Right here! To be able to pull all the puzzle pieces together, to use all that our scientists and academics had learned and shared for us to intentionally connect to streams of information that flow readily through and around us. Energy never dies. Information too is composed of energy. It is continuous and always present even when not seen by the naked eye. And the key to tapping into it is what we focus our attention and intention on at any given moment.

Imagine a massage therapist who prepares to touch their client. At the exact moment before the therapist lays hands on the client, they are overwhelmed with sadness and stress. The therapist knew they were fine before the client walked into the room, yet they were now faced with this overwhelming sense that their body was not well. Did it come from the therapist or the client? The answer: the client is carrying it in their fascia and musculature. What about a lion tamer who feels a chilly wave of energy pass through their brain and body before the lion they are trying to control swats at them in anger, giving them time to back away and not get hit by its huge claws? Or what about the sailboat captain who can smell weather trouble in the air, even on a sunny day? We get to choose what we want to focus on and the universe responds by continuously streaming information to us depending on our thoughts. Each of these examples needs to be examined further for the reasons why those people developed a specific skill set. Whatever it is that we focus on expands and contributes to our life experiences. If we learn a specific skill set, the universe conspires with us, affording us the experiences to become innately and intuitively aware.

The human body is the creator or shapeshifter of multiple realities based on our thought patterns, maintaining the ability to catch and release information like a radio system that carries information from place to place by processing signal waves. It is a powerful net that catches, filters, deciphers, and releases energy consistently. For example, the immune system keeps us healthy despite the plethora of organisms and toxic substances within our atmosphere, soil, foods, and water. It is but a microcosm within many macrocosms headed up by a universal consciousness that ebbs and flows throughout our lives. I know and experience the universal consciousness as a living, loving expression of all life that everyone and every living thing is capable of tapping into. We are all connected to it by this force, which is not visible to the naked eye per se, but instead, is sensed on much deeper levels by using a sixth or perhaps even a greater-than-sixth sense. This energetic life force lives within the cells and molecules of all matter, communicating every millisecond of each day. It surrounds us and communicates with all other energies within our space, shaping our experiences in this world and many others. How do I know this is true? **It is my life, my intentional focus,** and the information I share that reveals how a fully sentient being uses all innate and taught abilities to maintain and restore balance within the body, while also being able to connect with all things outside the body. You can, too! Everyone is made of the same stuff. With focus and intentionality, you can also harness the power to put it to work within your life. To me, harnessing such power means being able to weave a web of magic into everyday, ordinary life that you too will learn to trust. As you begin to trust what you sense, you will move beyond any semblance of normal living that you had experienced prior to today. You will experience the magical world that has been hiding inside and all around you. It knows all and it is ready and willing to share its knowledge with your conscious mind when you decide you are ready.

Embracing the Ideology ~ The State of Being

What does it take? It takes intentional focus and the desire to dig deeper, connect more deeply, or maybe even educate oneself more thoroughly.

Education and the expansion of human awareness, as well as caring for ourselves and aiding others in their efforts, are critical to the prevention and treatment of illness and the overall wellness, enlightenment, and attainment of the societies of the world. To remain healthy as we age in our seemingly toxic environments requires vigilance and conscious effort. The desire for humans to achieve is instinctive, and now more than ever, we multidimensional beings have the means to accelerate and fulfill our higher potential. To expand our awareness, we will begin by focusing our attention on cell communication. As I developed my sensory abilities, I chose to focus on developing a specific technique that would allow me to listen and communicate with the cells within my body or the cells within another person, as well as other living things. I use the technique both for me and for others. I use it just like a dolphin uses echolocation. The dolphin sends sound or energy out into the ocean to locate food or things. I send my energy out into the world while holding a question in my mind so that my energy can enter the body of another. I take a look around at the organs and systems, allowing myself to truly feel what that person or animal is experiencing.

With the use of all the techniques I have shared, my energy is allowed to move through space and time to visit clients all over the world without doing so physically, in person. I'm able to tap into someone else's realm of consciousness to gather and harvest information. Whether it is for self-education or to help my client, I am able to use my own sensory system to gain insight. I am able to feel someone else's pain, see the world through their eyes, and experience life as they perceive it.

It may be difficult for some to understand why any reasonable or prudent person would want to feel what someone else is feeling. My reason for doing it? A soft voice within me said this was necessary for my own growth and that I was to share what I learned. That voice provided the impetus that propelled me into my studies and encouraged me to aid humanity in shifting beyond its limited views. Furthermore, I truly understand who and what you are and how you have experienced the world around you. I hold you and your experiences in my heart with no judgment about your perceptions while holding the space for you to grow beyond any outmoded misconceptions that no longer serve you.

Can people abuse this kind of power? I prefer that this not happen, but the truth of the matter is that some may try. I have not had any personal experience with that happening. Those I know in the healing arts choose to do no harm. This is the unspoken golden rule amongst practitioners, so even though there is a possibility of people misusing what I am teaching, my desire is and will always be to focus on encouraging people to treat all living things as they wish to be treated. What energy you send out into the world comes back to you.

When sensory abilities are utilized properly, we can each begin to intimately understand how magical and profound life really is.

What is the ultimate payoff for me? I am always thinking seven generations ahead rather than thinking of a reward in the present. I am thinking about what I can do to make life better for the tribes that will inhabit the earth in the years to come. Using remote viewing techniques to probe the future of humanity revealed a world of peace for a thousand or more years. I'd love to be here for that!

Trust ~ It's Magical

I learned to trust the messages and information I was receiving.

My parents did not willfully teach me how to be intuitive. There just seemed to be something innate within me that instigated this particular life path. It has taken over thirty years to get really comfortable with my abilities. Now that I have been using them my entire life, I can honestly say that I would never want to be without them. My practices are intentional.

Now, open your own wormhole of intentionality. Begin by using creative imagery to open the door into your universal mind's eye. Take in a long, deep, refreshing breath and imagine that your body is a fisherman's net made up of intricately woven strands that drift silently through the universal waters of life. As the net drifts, it assesses tiny bits of information and isolates data that is pertinent to the questions you hold within your mind. Those finely woven strands are made up of cells that catch and filter the white noise and disseminate the information to all cells, tissues, organs, and systems within your body. The organelles within the cells then decide how they are going to manage the information—whether they translate the information and use it in-house or whether they send that information back out into the world.

You're an empath, too! I don't think you are reading this by accident. Your life and your experiences have brought you here. Just as nature allows an animal to develop specific traits to become more comfortable within its environment, for self-protection or to protect its young, your experiences have led you to your next growth spurt. As you begin to fully grasp what it actually means to be empathic, just know that you'll be tested time and time again. Well, maybe I should say that you'll get every opportunity to test your own abilities. The challenges will involve you being clear about what you want to focus on and how intentional your practice will be.

If you are going to play with the universe, be clear on what you want to know and what you want to experience. Then, hold on! Be impartial, be without prejudices, be mindful and intentionally focused on your target, then let your spirit fly free to connect more deeply.

There is more to life than meets the eye. The brain and the body of every living creature can see, hear, smell, taste, and feel beyond normal perceptions. Science, quantum physics more especially, teaches that the brain sees and understands far more than any one sensory organ does all by itself. What happens when fully sentient beings use every sensory structure afforded to them at birth?

Magic!

When you begin to see the magic, the puzzle pieces will come together naturally, and the *magical events will multiply*. When you truly *see*, those seemingly mystical or inexplicable experiences will turn an ordinary life into what fairy tales are made of. I am living proof and I'm willing to bet that you are, too.

Message from the Author

I offer my heartfelt appreciation for those who have chosen to be with me in this life, sharing, practicing, loving, laughing, and living. I offer my deepest condolences to those who have lost loved ones during the breaking down and building up that our world has endured. I see and feel you!

Throughout my existence, I've had ample time to consider what life is really about. Some days, while watching the chaos unfold in the world around me, I've caught myself thinking a disempowering thought: *From womb to tomb, our lives are not our own*. Then, I remind myself how my thoughts or perceptions shape my experiences. If I had no control over my life, then I'd create experiences that confirmed I was a slave to someone or something outside my being. The thought, *our lives are not our own*, creates a sense of powerlessness. It's mind/body pollution! Identifying it was the first step I took toward changing my life. It helped me shift my thinking and reshape the way in which I wanted to live my life from then on. Whether I welcomed the inner pollution or I consciously took control to create inspiring thought forms, the universal energies-that-be provided experiences that would either confirm my beliefs or nullify them.

Can it really be that easy to change your life? Let's *see*.

Most consider the word *see* in terms of its dictionary definition, in which it is defined as having the ability to perceive with the eyes, to discern visually, discern or deduce mentally after reflection or upon receiving information. My interpretation as it pertains to my life work purposefully conveys a deeper meaning, one of understanding. When we truly understand, we're capable of unconditionally loving all life forms and living each day in compassionate acceptance. For me, knowing what I know has been liberating.

For the sake of total transparency, I had chosen a different title for this work. *SEE* had been a labor of love and transformation that began with my personal compilation of true-life experiences bridging science with intuition, yet as I finalized everything for publishing, the title just did not fit. Everything about this life and my experiences had to do with showing humans how extraordinary life can be when we evolve into higher states of consciousness. Sharing my life had nothing to do with ringing my own bell. I had watched people give their power away and gain nothing by losing themselves to the authority of others. Throughout this process SEE went through a metamorphosis just as we all do throughout our lives. As I woke on January 1, 2024, SEE had evolved into EVOLUTIO, the Latin root of Evolution, meaning "to unroll like a scroll." EVOLUTIO was to provide the keys that unravel or unroll the scroll of life by bridging science and intuition, without making it difficult for everyone to understand. You don't have to be an academic to understand all of this. The storytelling has been added to make it easier to realize one's own power and apply these principles to everyday life, thereby raising humanity and accelerating human potential. Since completing numerous edits over many years EVOLUTIO evolved yet again into THE ART OF PEACE. While meditating on where to publish this book I was reminded of my first book and the intentionality of empowering humanity to use their inherent gifts for inner and outer peace. There's an art to honing sensory abilities and with repeated practice it becomes natural to use them for everything, always. Furthermore, man has perfected war. Now it is time for us all to rise to the challenge of perfecting peace.

All along there had been a knowledge that it was time for humans to release the old and evolve into the new, which had been an ongoing message for me as well. It was evident I had to make some changes before publishing. Where SEE was more so about understanding all life forms, EVOLUTIO unravels the true meaning of life, unifies all life forms and shifts perceptions, which is necessary for the world ahead and the generations to come. THE ART OF PEACE raises humanity to new heights, unifying us with every living thing on Earth and beyond.

Where Nicole Myers was born an empathic warrioress that wanted to stop all suffering, kick ass and take names, and Nicole Myers Henderson wanted to understand why humans choose to suffer and cause suffering. The old me had carried the weight of the world and the suffering of others on her shoulders. Today, I want to live free, love deeply, connect and engage in loving ways with all life forms. Understanding the message, I now am able to give myself permission to change. Out with the old, in with the new, and there I found myself anew. There was no need for me to carry the weight of the world on my empathic shoulders or fix everyone's woes. THE ART OF PEACE is to change all of that, not just for me but for all other empaths, lightworkers, and anyone who feels more deeply and has the desire to be at one with all life on this planet and beyond.

Note, as you immerse yourself into the text that in several instances I chose to change the names of those who I shared my experiences with to protect their privacy, yet all else remains as it was and as the experiences unfolded. The rest consists of years of research, compiled information, and puzzle pieces, all pulled together for you to digest and apply to your own life, for your own conscious evolution.   *Namaste*

I close my eyes; my brain can SEE

Stone Mountain in North Carolina calls and draws us back to her every couple of years so that my husband can test himself. Since his diagnosis of Parkinson's over twenty-five years ago, he likes to gauge its progression while also holding the vision to beat it; never allowing it to beat him. To him, that mountain, friend or foe, helps him determine whether the disease is robbing him of his faculties or whether the mountain and nature can offer solace. Being in nature, climbing on, up, over, and around the mountain afforded him a positive challenge that, time and time again, allowed him to rise, grow, and heal.

Together, we enjoy the walks, not only to reinforce my husband's desire to live longer, but also to quiet my own body, mind, and spirit. My empathic work takes a lot out of me, and I love the quiet time it offers to ground and release whatever it is that might be consuming me.

With each visit, I notice that my relationship with the mountain deepens. It feels as if the mountain opens or reveals herself to me, allowing me to tap into the life forms that scurry, play, drift, and nestle into her every nook and cranny. She shares that many visitors overlook the life on and within the mountain, my husband included. He visits with his own mission or agenda, and there isn't a need to feel what the mountain experiences. Many see the mountain yet don't truly *SEE* the treasures or magic within and around her. But I do.

On occasion, our grandson, Izaiah, would join in on our adventures. On this particular visit, he had just turned four. He was at *that* age where there were more questions than answers, and he paid attention to every little thing that went on around him, which meant that I had to work to maintain the bubble of silence I so dearly loved during such hikes.

We typically parked and started our walks on the lower part of Stone Mountain Park; however, this time, we decided to leave our vehicle in the top lot. Everything excited Izaiah, and the more he learned, the happier he was. He loved to explore, so we had to be sure he listened to us when we told him to be careful, to listen when we knew the stones would give way, tree limbs and roots might prove challenging, or the soil might shift under his feet. Watching him and the way he formed his own thoughts based on the information we shared was exciting. How he chose to respond to the first part of the hike gave us time to determine whether he could make the hike back to the car.

From the parking area to the mountain top, my grandson trotted back and forth between my husband and me, barely able to contain himself. One minute, he'd be holding Monty's hand, helping him keep his footing. The next, he'd run back to walk and talk with me. Everything he saw sparked a new question. Every leaf, rock, and critter made him laugh, sing, or beg for more information, and according to him, I was the key to getting those answers.

"Mom-mom! Why are you so quiet?"

"I love my quiet time on these hikes, Zay."

"Why?"

"Because everything speaks to me out here. Kind of like the questions you're asking me, I speak to the Earth and ask her questions. When I'm quiet, I'm listening to see whether the wind, water, rocks, insects, birds, or animals will answer."

His eyes grew wide and as if transfixed by my statement, his mouth hung open, awe oozing from every stitch of his being. "Na-uh! How do you do that? How do you talk to all those things? Are they talking to you now?" My husband stopped dead in his tracks and buckled over, laughing, where he couldn't be seen or heard by the nagging toddler.

"Well Zay, I have to be incredibly quiet. If I fill the space with lots of talk, I can't hear them. So, I stay quiet and think of questions I want answers to. Then, I send my questions out to see what or who will answer them. Imagine that you and Pop-pop are going fishing. You need a fishing pole, fishing line, a hook, and some worms. You put a worm on your hook and cast the line out into the water. Then, you wait for the fish to take the bait. When I talk to the mountain, my questions are like that worm on a hook. I think of my question and cast the line out into the universal waters. When the answers are on the hook, I feel it. I pull the line in to examine the fish I caught. In this case, the fish is the answer to the question I asked."

"I want to do that! Teach me!"

"Honey, that takes lots of practice and you have to be quiet. So far, you haven't shown me that you can hold your tongue for more than a few seconds. If you keep talking, you'll never hear what anyone or anything else has to say."

"What do you hear Mom-mom? What are you listening to? What are they saying to you?"

My husband, hearing the conversation, gave me a solid nod to show that he liked what we were talking about. With eyes locked on him, I answered, "I don't know, Zay. You've been talking so much I can't hear the answers. If you can be quiet for a few minutes, I might be able to tell you."

In full trot and dancing in circles, he began to sing, "**Life is a highway, I'm gonna drive it all night long**." Then, he paused, turned to me, and said, "Okay, I can do that!" He ran to catch up to Monty, and all I could hear was his chipmunk voice telling him all about our conversation.

We managed to get to the base of the mountain, yet still not in quiet. Zay danced back and forth between the two of us with the energy of fifty men. I held my tongue, watching him, leaving him to play, and when Monty stopped to find a tree to relieve himself, Zay followed, amused that he was allowed to drop his britches to pee in the woods.

Words filled the air with every step he took. I couldn't help but smile inwardly, and like a moth drawn to a flame, Zay fluttered back to me.

"Mom-mom are you still talking to them?" his arm outstretched, waving at the trees, and pointing to the dirt at his feet.

"Yes, I am."

"Well...what are they saying?" Feet trotting in place, eyes sparkling, he repeated eagerly, "What are they saying?"

"The trees say that we need to hurry to get over the mountain. It's going to rain." I closed my eyes and drew a deep breath. "Yep! It's going to rain. The trees all say so."

"NO WAY! Look at the sky! It's beautiful out here. The sun is shining. It's not going to rain. They're wrong!"

"Well, Zay...I don't doubt what they're telling me. They don't lie. They said that we will have just enough time to get up and over that mountain, get you back to the car, and just as we do that, the sky is going to let loose." His little legs couldn't carry him fast enough to catch up to his grandfather.

"Pop-pop! Mom-mom is talking to the trees, and they tell her it's going to rain. Do you believe that?"

"Yes, son. Mom-mom talks to things you and I can't. Like she said, they don't lie to her, and I have no reason to doubt what she just told you. So, we'd better listen and get over this mountain." Zay reached for Monty's hand.

"Well then, you better let me help you get up these stairs. I am stronger than you. We can hurry, but only if I carry you," Izaiah said.

I raised my eyebrows and smiled as Monty made eye contact with me. He called back, "This kid's amazing!"

My husband maneuvered the stairs pretty well, but not without having to stop a number of times to catch his breath. Zay patiently stood by him each time. Before starting the next set of stairs, he'd run ahead to scout out how difficult the climb might be for Monty, then run back to offer his superior strength to manage the next set of stairs. As we crested the top, Zay noticed the sky starting to darken. "Mom-mom, you might be right," I smirked but didn't respond. "Come on, Pop-pop, we need to get to the car."

Hiking gear loaded into the trunk and Zay in his car seat, I snapped on his seatbelt as the first drops started to fall. We leaped into the front seats when it started pouring and laughter filled the car.

"Mom-mom, I want to do what you do. I want to talk to the trees. Can you teach me?

"Yes."

"I watched you. When you are doing it, you close your eyes. Why do you do that?"

"Well, like today, you were being very noisy. When there's a lot going on around me, and I need to focus past all the noise, I close my eyes so that my brain can see."

With a smile on his face, he laid his head back and closed his eyes. Monty watched him in the rearview mirror. "Son, if you like hiking with us, where would you like to go next?"

"I don't know yet, Pop-pop. Let me close my eyes so my brain can see."

Chapter One

Milestones

The magical journey of the living is jam-packed with milestones. Often, they mysteriously occur, provoking the most growth. The big ones change the trajectory of our life. I recall experiencing more than my fair share of the big ones that seemed to come at me out of nowhere; however, more often than not, I'd chosen or provoked the growth myself. Change became my constant companion. My perspective and emotional reactions determined what change would come next.

With each major milestone, I had a choice as to whether I would act or be reactive. I could let my emotions boil over and lose myself, or I could choose the path of the peaceful warrioress, which always led to more enlightenment. Seeing my choices as either good or bad meant little. I learned to be mindful of how I framed my thoughts. I got to decide what I was going to focus on and if I experienced less than desirable results, I still got to choose what would take up space in my brain. So, no matter the milestone, perceived as positive or negative, any experience could boil down to my own *perspective*. If an experience provided negative results, I could shift my thinking and choose to initiate another experience. Each taught me something, allowing me to grow beyond my old ways and outmoded thought forms. I learned to ask better questions and look for solutions, rather than fixate on problems. Perspective is the key to living a magical life, full of sensory-rich experiences and the further development of innate spiritual gifts with which each and every one of us is born.

All life, all energy, through all dimensions is conscious, aware, and evolving.

Note: Bear in mind that there are many forms of energy, from the largest forms to fundamental particles, the building blocks of atomic nuclei. We would traverse many different rabbit holes if I mentioned them here. I'll ask that you keep an open mind as you read, knowing that we'll be touching on the keystones to living conscious, science, and intuition, rather than fine-tuning or tuning into specific business or life practices. Just know that by using the techniques I share here, you can go down any rabbit hole you want. You'll get to decide how you use what you learn.

Every living thing evolves according to its environment. For me, sometimes, there were seemingly insignificant evolutionary changes, and other times, monumental leaps in consciousness. For the whole of humanity, I'd say we're in the midst of some doozies right now. What our mind, body, and spirit once tolerated will not be tolerated for much longer, and as this next great leap in consciousness takes place, absolute trust will be needed. If you feel like a big square peg being forced into a tiny round hole, everything about you from the inside out will be forced into changing, growing, and evolving even more than you already have. As you stretch past any breaking point you thought you had, I'd like for you to remember that you have a choice. Choose whether you feel better when you **react** to life experiences or feel best when you have chosen to *act* in concert with life events. Each time you *act with* life, you cement-in a deeper level of trust and inner knowing that something bigger than yourself knows better, and that's when the magic happens.

Now, take a deep breath. Get some fresh air into that beautiful brain and body of yours. That's it. BREATHE.

Before you read any further, take a moment to assess where you are right now. How you feel. What you might be fixated on. It's important for you to know whether you trust yourself. Do you use and trust your intuition? Do you feel better thinking that there's a higher power at work in your life? Do you feel connected to that higher power right now? Write down your answers and take notes as you read. Make note of any life-changing milestones you're reminded of.

Chapter Two

Trusting My Intuition

I t was 2005 when I heard a small, stilling voice telling me to write. Then 2014 when I published what I had written in ON SACRED TIME Tapping the Power Within. I shared the key to unlocking the power, your cellular memory genius, that resides within the cells of every living thing, guiding those willing souls to trust the connection to the source of all life.

Drafting that book was a milestone for me, and if you read it, you may recall that I had some pretty amazing experiences that shaped me into the person I am today. Some good experiences and many bad. Through the process, I was able to clear the toxic emotions that burdened my physical body. Physical ailments seemed to mysteriously disappear once I understood the intelligence within my cells, and as I surmounted each milestone, I deepened my perception and developed a broader perspective; an eye-opening universal perspective; that unified all things rather than separated them. That unifying perspective is what sparked the events you'll read about now.

I wouldn't consider my life seven years ago to be as complex as it is now. Now, it's 2024 and post-pandemic. It appears that life for everyone is more complicated, yet in another sense, less. Things I was told would happen while in meditation so many years ago have come to pass, offering confirmation of the profound changes that have taken place. Now, we're three-plus years past the 2020 Covid-19 pandemic release and I'm being led to share more with you. There's still craziness in the air. I admit, I'm unsettled at times, although I continue to receive information that suggests there are better days ahead. I *sense* better days ahead. If you don't feel or see that right now, I trust that something shared here will lead you to a deeper understanding, balance, and inner peace.

THE ART OF PEACE is an accumulation of my business and firsthand experiences combined with research, theories, and discoveries that date back to before Albert Einstein. As I edit and re-edit, the memories are rich and colorful, inspiring, and mind-altering. I'm grateful Great Spirit chose me to live this life. I pray each day to experience more of the magic and it's my hope that if you don't already know it, you'll come to understand that intuition is more than mysterious, uncontrollable, or as the doubting-Thomas might call "woo-woo." It's been my beliefs, as well as my personal experience, which validate that intuition does not stand apart from science; that by integrating science and intuition, humanity can take the next evolutionary leap that allows for the merging of all universal puzzle pieces, unifying our fragmented lives into one big masterpiece.

Today, believe me when I say, YOU ARE amazing, beautiful, and perfect! You deserve to know how powerful you are. With what's happening in the world today, expanding your knowledge and putting puzzle pieces together will help you fall madly in love with life, even when all hell breaks loose around you. Through good and tough times, we should take a stand based on truth, band together, and not allow ourselves to be ripped apart, segregated. Knowing more can foster unity-mindedness and solidify a highly evolved global society that embraces its power for the good of all.

We all have a superpower that we each were born with to put to effective use. My intuition, my ability to stream and decipher information at a microscopic scale from the multiverse, to see the bigger picture, is my superpower. I see things most people can't, or simply choose not to.

Do you know what your superpower is?

WHEN YOU CHANGE YOUR THOUGHTS, YOU CHANGE YOUR LIFE

As I mentioned earlier, much of the change and growth I experienced early in my life was totally unexpected. It wasn't until much later in life that I realized I possessed the power to change my future by merely aligning myself with the joy I would experience when I could see myself *in action with* whatever it is that I am thinking about. That I can, in the midst of a crisis, shift my thoughts and turn a disagreeable situation into something absolutely amazing. Sustaining such abilities took lots of practice. It still does when I am distracted by other things. I had to repeat the things that worked for me and develop the muscle memory to continue doing it again and again. Each experience led to the mastering of my senses.

Telling you that mastering intuition takes practice reminds me of something my husband, a trained law enforcement officer, said. Knowing this has helped me stay open to learning more, while also being more patient with myself and others. He said, "In order for an officer to be fully prepared to pull a firearm in the midst of danger, they have to practice pulling that gun three thousand times so that when they do have to use it, it won't take any thought. It will be an automatic response to a threatening situation." So, whether you want to change something about your life, learn something new, or break an old habit, it takes practice. Consider doing it three thousand times purposefully so that one day, it will be instinctual. It's also helpful when someone else models a behavior I want to adopt. By watching someone else do what you want to do, it gives you ample time to learn what's possible.

Let my life be the example that shows you how to tap into the power of you, to *SEE* this innate power within all things.

Chapter Three

How We've Learned

I imagine man has always had to grapple with his own fears, along with the fears of the panic-peddlers of the world. A caveman plundering for food as a huge shadow floats across the sky above him. He shakes and shudders as he rushes back to the cave to share his fears with the clan. They, too, shudder at every large shadow that streaks across the sky now, although they have not seen it for themselves.

How is it possible that one man's fear, his perception of an experience, to trickle like water through his tribe, wreaking havoc, even when they themselves never saw or experienced what he did? That's the world today!

THE SKY IS FALLING! THE SKY IS FALLING! Right?

Often, we don't have to experience something ourselves. We listen to snippets of a story, chock-full of someone else's perception that's being handed down to us. Then, when we empathize with their emotions.

Take a moment and let whatever old stories or memories that were shared with you over the years that you didn't have personal experience with the surface. What shows up? Maybe Grandma, Grandpa, Mom, Dad, or someone else close to you shared a negative experience. Did you get caught up in their story? Have you been fearful of those things happening to you? Do you feel manipulated by their story? Consider that our reactions to someone else's experiences are trillions of years in the making. Human manipulates human. Human overpowers human. Human fears human and the world around them. Other humans feel forlorn, dejected, disempowered, and beaten down by experiences they never had. The stories and someone else's fears were handed down from generation to generation. And today, amid the Covid-19 pandemic and seemingly scarce resources, the unaware, disconnected, and already inflamed portion of society grows restless, fearfully waiting to see what's next.

Do we settle into the panic-peddling? Accept what someone else says is true? Follow someone else's lead or find a better way to live our own lives? Can we look at life and the history of humans to *see* the beauty that's all around us, even when others teach us through their storytelling that life is hard, painful, and ugly?

Bottom line: It's easy to get caught up in and drawn deeper into someone's negativity. It's easy to be at odds with or to go to war over the things we don't like, instead of gathering together to spark change and growth.

War. There's another age-old tradition. Man has perfected war, and man knows that with a little panic-peddling wars can be started quickly to control and manipulate the masses. Those in power positions prefer to lead us to dark places so that we become dependent upon them. They prefer we not change or learn to think for ourselves. They prefer we stay the same; stuck in our negative emotions. Enslaved by our fears. Or, enslaved by their fears. Not changing is easy, right? Not changing provides some level of comfort, yes? So, why change? Because settling gets old and so does blaming others for our choices, especially when we think we're being forced to make them. We've worn it out, and if you don't want to live life that way any longer, then it's time to shift your perspective. The fact remains that it's your life. It's your choice.

Even when you don't feel like you have a choice, there are always other opportunities available. When armed with this knowledge, you can choose what's right for you. You can choose to awaken that special something inside you and find your own answers, and now is the perfect time to awaken your inner sight, to *SEE* the magic of life and **the magic in you**.

Chapter Four

Perceiving the SHIFT!

B eing here in this time can indicate that you've either had some magical experiences that you can't explain, or you're in the dark thinking about how trivial and painful life seems to be. Day in and day out, you get out of bed, tend to chores, delve into work, lunch, more work, traffic, shopping, kids, parents, house, bills, the yard and garden, pets, dinner, and on a macro-scale, politics, or the news to catch up on world affairs. Then, you feel the need to shower or bathe to clean the negative energy off of your body and out of your mind. After feeling thoroughly drained, it's off to bed, only to do it all over again the very next day. The mere thought of how full and overwhelming one day can be, may bring bouts of depression, anxiety, and stress. Add self-induced pressure to do right and avoid doing wrong. We're on adrenal overload and more often than not, we do it to ourselves!

So...where's the magic in life if your life is framed the way I wrote it above? What's life really about?

Let's break it down.

Chapter Five

Natural or Supernatural

*I*t's often what we cannot see with our eyes that holds the most power.

All living things possess what *seems* to be a supernatural ability to intuitively sense things. Consider the following examples.

Early, in human development, even the cave dweller had experiences with intuition. Imagine, as he starts his day in search of food for the clan, he gets a chill and has this overwhelming sensation; a sense of impending danger, just moments before he is swept off his feet by a large prehistoric raptor. Or...

While readying for bed, a Native American shaman prays for his tribe as he seeks answers from the Great Spirit. While praying, his mind is able to shape-shift his being into the form of a wolf, which allows him to walk the perimeter of a US Calvary camp to hear how the military plans to attack his tribe the very next day. By seeing and hearing within his wolf-like vision, he's able to wake the tribe, evacuate, and save their lives. Or...

A twin living in North Carolina feels a sharp pain in her right pointer finger as her sister, who lives in Michigan, cuts the exact finger down to the bone with a knife.

Are these freak incidents or natural occurrences?

I have spent years in deep contemplation about this, asking questions like, *what is* responsible for our intuitive urgings? Is it something inside us that provokes these experiences, or is it something outside us, within our environment? Is it really a psychic experience that cannot be explained, or has science already revealed its secrets? Can the brain and sensory network be responsible for intuitive urgings?

I think, sometimes, it's more exciting to believe that these events are mystical. Many people experience intuitive hits and they seem perfectly happy not knowing how they do it or where those hits come from. How often do you hear people talk about knowing what their spouse was about to say before they said it? How often have you had an experience with knowing who is on the other end of the phone when it rings? We all, at one point in our lives, have experienced intuition in one way or another.

Over the past decade, advancements within the fields of neuroscience, quantum theory/physics, energy transference, and cell communication (within all living things) have helped us better understand the complexities or connections associated with our neural network, sensory organs, *and* how our environment acts with the ebb and flow of our thoughts. The sensory structures within all living things have developed over time, allowing for natural, or organic evolutionary processes to occur.

Where are we now?

We've made it through the New Age movement, where we were taught that intuition was linked to paranormal and metaphysical experiences that were thought to be of spiritual or religious origin and practices. Some say some people are born with *it* and some say not. I say we all have *it*. *It just* needs to be nurtured.

In addition, throughout the New Age wave, scientists made great strides in documenting the structures of the human body and how the energy within our cells connects to not just the universe, but the multiverses. I am particularly excited when I read over works dating back to Einstein about the unified field theory, as well as successfully documented theories that other scientists share from before and after the 1800s. Even more exciting are developments that have come to light more recently that let us glue (in a sense) new and old information together.

When we intentionally amalgamate old theories with new puzzle pieces shared by modern-day physicists, cosmologists, and experts in other fields, we transcend old paradigms of thought, thoughts that are self-limiting, that hold us back. Thoughts that unfavorably influence our behavior, causing us to believe that we are at the whim and will of an unseeable force. Believing that leaves us feeling as if we are reliant only upon outside authorities and agencies to make decisions that can have longstanding negative effects on our lives and those we care for. God says do this. Mother says don't do that because. Husband says that's not true; you need to believe *me*, not *them*. Lawyer says her way is the only way. Doctor says don't do that; you'll hurt yourself. Trust me. Government says you must do it my way. Do you get my point?

Are we lambs being led to slaughter or just lazy? Neither.

Maybe you feel inadequate. Maybe you don't think you're capable of making your own decisions. Perhaps you weren't taught that there is an infinitely knowledgeable intuitive genius residing within the cells of your body that can answer every question you'll ever have.

But what happens when you can't connect with that knowledge-able genius? You end up believing that someone or something else is in control of your life and you give your power away. Maybe it's easier to believe in someone or something else. Maybe it makes you feel better to blame something else for your own inadequacies, your own laissez-faire-like ways or your hands-off attitude. You're not alone. We all have our moments. When we feel stripped of our power, we have someone or something else to blame when things go wrong. Fact is, as many quantum thinkers have revealed in recent years, our thoughts create things! Good thoughts or bad thoughts, it doesn't matter. What matters is what we feel when we're thinking about what we want or don't want. Our thoughts are fuel for the universal mind.

The universe, being a feeling universe, doesn't care if you want or don't want something. What it cares about is its strong connection to feelings that are linked to the images that you created in your mind. It's the strong emotions that feed the desire to expand or contract energy.

Good or bad, the universe feels and feeds on your thoughts. The secret is, it prefers to feel and feed joy-filled thoughts.

Are you holding any negative thoughts about intuition? Before moving on, take a few moments to tune-in to any old story that might show up for review. Get in touch with any strong emotions you might have about those stories. Your emotions will trigger what you'll experience as you read more. Take note of any strong negative feelings you might have about the labels people have placed on seers. Historically, free thinkers, psychics, clairvoyants, clairsentients, clairaudients, intuitives, witches, shamans, call them whatever you like, have been feared. Their gifts couldn't be explained, and not knowing how they do it provokes fear. If you are afraid of them, park your judgment. I can't tell you how many times I have heard people say that they're afraid of people with such abilities, and when they themselves experience such things, it freaks them out to the point of shutting down or running away. Many underdeveloped empaths have called me to say they are ready to check out because they can't stomach what they're feeling. And in most cases, what they were feeling had nothing to do with them. What they were feeling was not coming from inside them; it was coming at them, and their body was acting like a net, catching, processing, and deciphering the intel.

Without understanding how you receive, send, or decipher information can be just as daunting, and can make you feel as if your life is spiraling out of control.

I hope to allay any fears you might have about this topic.

Intuition is not something to fear, but instead, should be embraced and nurtured. It is a brain process that cooperates with the cellular structure of the body to measure inside and outside stimuli, which affords us the ability to make decisions without the use of analytical reasoning, and the big news is... anyone and everything has this inner knowing. Each living thing is innately self-controlled and self-guided, and each living thing is able to interact with everything outside itself.

You know those trillions of cells that make up your entire body? They're jam-packed with power. They are free-thinking! They don't need input from our conscious mind. And we are not at the whim and will of an unseen current. The cells of our body dance with the atoms, molecules, and particles of all other living things. And our thoughts and beliefs create what we will experience as our life dance continues.

Chapter Six

Living a Sensory Life ~ Full Awareness

E xperiences with intuition began at an incredibly early age for me. My mother made mention of a few haunted houses we had lived in while I was a baby, although I only remember having conscious awareness of seeing and feeling the presence of spirits beginning at the age of four. As I reminisce, I remember how my body responded to the stimulation. During each instance, my hair would stand on end and my body would become rigid, as if frozen in one spot when the spirits moved around me. It always scared me, and amazingly, still gives me goosebumps to this day, although I feel better equipped to handle them now. At first, I chose not to tell anyone; then, when I was old enough to understand what was happening, I began to share the bone-chilling experiences with those I felt I could trust.

Seeing spirits went on for some time without knowing what they wanted from me, until something shifted within me in my late teens. I had experienced several accidents, often spurred on by my brothers or friends. I've had motorcycle wrecks, falling off horses, and fistfights provoked by the simple-minded who love to cause pain and suffering. I'd been molested, date-raped, been physically beaten by someone who said they loved me while they were pointing a gun in my face, threatening my life. Trauma from each episode could have triggered something in my brain to act differently, yet I'd rather believe that it was a compilation of those events that sparked a shift in my cells or changed my thoughts about how I wanted to live my life. I knew I wanted to live differently, and it was that in-depth focus and intention that caused the deeper shift that led me to take my first leap forward. As I held the focus to change, **something** else seemed to have designed a path that I was meant to follow. A new life began to reveal itself, and any negative experiences I had prior provided an incentive to stay on track and not go back to my old ways. Each shift told me that I had reached a milestone that would birth another shift. I was destined to change and grow beyond any of my mundane thoughts and painful experiences.

My early interactions with the spirit realm allowed me to see spirits and see their mouths moving, but I couldn't hear any words. Then, my perception shifted to seeing them and hearing their words. With years of practice and intuitive development, I stopped seeing them, and instead, could feel them and hear or sense their words. Much like one senses the wind on a breezy day, I was being communicated with in a deeper, more meaningful way. I could feel them. I could feel things about their life. Empathizing with them often meant that I would have to endure the pain and sadness they had experienced, or their death, which often tested my resolve and consumed my life.

Empathizing also brought bigger issues as I got older. Feeling the energy of the dead wasn't my only worry. Dealing with the feelings of those living around me brought just as much pain and sadness. I remember my mother telling friends and family that I was a hypochondriac when I was about six or seven years old. She said that I was always feeling bad and complaining about something. It wasn't until my later teens and into my early twenties that those childhood pains made perfect sense. Rather than being a hypochondriac, I came to realize that I was extremely empathic—deeply intuitive. I remember always feeling that life was a struggle when spirits or other people were around. The times leading up to my mother and father's divorce were particularly horrific. I felt better on the days when I was able to slink off to sit quietly with the neighbor's dogs. Spending time out in nature or with my animal friends often made me feel better, until around the age of nine, when deep feelings of sadness wafted through me each time I stopped to pet our neighbor's dog.

Chapter Seven

Entanglement

S he was a beautiful black and white Portuguese water dog that spent her life chained to her doghouse, not far from her human family's residence. Known to be gregarious by nature, these fun and family-loving dogs are also great with children. Imagine taking a dog that, by nature, is such a wonderful spirit and prone to play, and confining it, stripping it of its freedom and happy-by-nature attitude, and breaking its spirit by minimizing its social interactions.

I looked forward to our daily visits, and we each made the most of our time together. As time passed, each visit became more difficult for me to endure as my energy became entangled with hers. I felt like she was dying inside. With each visit came deeper sadness, until one snowy day, she broke free of her chain and was hit by a car. At the exact moment she was hit, I was sitting on the floor of our living room watching television with my brothers. My nine-year-old body felt the impact and I heard her cry out to me. Barefoot and without winter clothing, I ran out to join her on the snow-covered road. I held her as blood ran from her ears and eyes. Heartbroken, I watched as her owner marched from his front doorstep with a gun. He walked to my side and pulled me from her, yelling, "Get away!" I screamed for him to stop as my mother came running from our house to pull me out of the road. I can still hear my own screams.

She was shot in the head twice and still managed to scramble to her feet to run to my side as my mother dragged me home. Her owner chased her and cornered her on our next-door neighbor's porch, putting a few extra .22 bullets into her body. My screams held her attention and she never took her eyes off me, nor did I lose sight of her. I heard the thud of her body as it mixed with blood and snowy slush. As she hit the ground one final time, I heard the air escape from her lungs; her eyes stayed fixed on me. I remember thinking in that instant that I would never trust an adult ever again.

***

At ten years old, I spent the summer on my best friend's farm playing and helping with their horses, dogs, cats, and cows. On one warm summer morning, I hung on the barnyard fence watching my best friend and her brother-in-law bottle-feed a newborn calf that was unable to nurse from its mother. As I turned my attention away from the soft, cuddly nursing calf and onto its mother, a dark yet thick meandering pain traveled through the frontal lobe of my brain, causing a sick feeling in my stomach. The cow was angry, and my body knew it. Sensing something was about to happen, I yelled out to Evelyn to tell her to get out of the barnyard. She turned to look at me, smiled, and shrugged, as if dismissing my concern just as the mother cow leaped on top of her, striking her in the back of the neck and head, bucking forward and back like an angry bull trying to get a cowboy off its back. Evelyn's eyes were as big as saucers as she tried to escape the cows' pounding hooves. The pain in my head and the sick feelings that registered within my body tipped me off to what was about to happen, but there was nothing I could do to stop it. Fortunately, her brother-in-law jumped in to snatch her from under the cow's hooves just before she was struck again.

In my mid-twenties, I began working with families and the police to find missing children. I could have never imagined that I would be able to do such things. I could feel what each victim had gone through in life, as well as what they endured during their death experience. I spent countless hours obsessing over the lives lost, never really feeling as if I had made an ounce of difference. Their experiences flowed through the cells of my body, making it difficult to focus or think about living my own life. I spent three years lost in sadness and pain, pondering my own mortality because of the deaths of those I was trying to help. Fearing I would lose myself, I chose to step away from that work, although I quickly learned that there was no way to truly escape. I would have to learn how to use my abilities in a totally unique way.

***

In my late twenties, my father introduced me to the NASCAR industry where he and his team spent hundreds of thousands of dollars and hour upon hour, warily getting their cars ready for weekly races. One day while hanging out with the team in their garage stall, the hum and vibration of the racecar engines lulled me into a meditative-like state. I closed my eyes and leaned on the racecar to take the load off my aching feet. The engine builder and crew chief were tweaking the jets in the motor to try to pick up the pace on the track, trying to make certain the driver would qualify to run the big Sunday race. I could hear the guys talking, mulling over scenarios that might give the driver what he needed out of the car. I remember thinking about not knowing much about racecars, but my lack of knowledge was soon replaced by my desire to help. While thinking about the motor and any potential engine issues, a virtual map of the inner workings of the car appeared in my mind's eye. Entirely by accident, a new world opened to me, creating a huge chasm between what I thought I knew to be true about life and a new, unsettling perspective that would fracture any semblance of normal I had previously experienced. How did I stumble into this virtual world? What did I do that I had not done before? I retraced my steps.

By leaning against the car and focusing on helping the team make the race, the car somehow answered my thoughts. What appeared in my mind's eye was a picture of the engine linked to a mishmash of electrical wires that ran from the motor down the center of the car within the driver's compartment. My heartbeat quickened as I heard an electric-like spark, which then suddenly faded just as I felt the engine lose power. Since this was my first experience with seeing, hearing, and feeling a racecar, I did not trust the information, so instead of sharing what I saw and heard, I chose to keep the experience to myself. As the team worked harder and faster to get ready, I forgot that it had happened.

That afternoon, the team ran their qualifying round and managed to place at the back of Sunday's racing field. Making the race calmed everyone's fears including my own, which made it easier to forget what had happened earlier that day.

Sunday came quickly. It was a sunny but cool morning at Darlington Motor Speedway in South Carolina when their driver took command of the Active Motorsports #32 Winston Cup racecar. Team members suited up and headed onto the track for driver introductions. As my father headed to the race hauler to watch the race, he handed me a headset and motioned for me to put it on so that I could hear the team and driver interactions. I wandered off to find an out-of-the-way spot to watch the race. Midway through, I felt a spike in my energy along with a quickening of my heartbeat. Without provocation, I began to hear the same spark-like sound that I had heard when I was leaning against the racecar in the garage the day before. I started to feel anxious, wondering where the sound was coming from. At one point, I got so freaked out by the energy that I couldn't swallow the saliva in my mouth. As I heard the noise repeat, I felt the motor lose power. My heart began to race so fast that I thought I was going to pass out. Then, something within me started putting the pieces together. I realized that the sound had to do with engine power and the energy dying off was the racecar losing power. I was so scared. I began to walk away from the racetrack when the driver's voice sounded over the headset.

"I've lost power and I don't know why."

"Try to get her started again," barked the crew chief.

The voices fell silent for a second; then, the driver keyed the mic. "Nothing, she won't start," the driver insisted as other racecars passed him on the track.

At that exact moment, a vision of the car map appeared in my mind's eye again, just like it had on Saturday before their qualifying run. It showed me the same tangle of wires that ran down the center of the car, but this time, it revealed that they ran into a box positioned to the right of the driver. I could see that a wire had come loose from the power box. For a millisecond, I thought about keying up the mic to tell the driver where to look. Then, apprehension set in.

Fearing how the team would react to my interference, I hesitated; then, I realized that by speaking up, I might help them finish the race. I moved to click in to tell the driver to check for a disconnected wire to the power box, and just as I touched the button, the driver keyed in and spoke.

"The wire to the power box is disconnected. I got it!" he yelled. He quickly reconnected the wire and fired the engine just in time to finish the race.

So, how did this happen? I lean on the car, and it shows up in my mind like an X-ray or MRI image. Interestingly, this was not my first experience with a technique known as psychometry, although it was my first truly life-enhancing and transformative encounter.

Chapter Eight

Psychometry

My research yielded that psychometry, aka psychoscopy, is a form of extrasensory perception characterized by the ability to make sensible or logical associations derived from making physical contact with an animated or inanimate object. Joseph Rodes Buchanan coined the word in 1842 when he came up with the notion that all things give off an emanation. "*The past is entombed in the present,*" said Buchanan in 1843, believing that all things of this world are an enduring monument. In 1885, he published the second edition of the *Manual of Psychometry: The Dawn of a New Civilization,* in which he detailed how direct knowledge of psychometry would be applied to and affect many branches of science, elevate schools of philosophy and art, and further influence wide social change by enlightening humanity. Psychometry is seen to be a measuring instrument or measure of power that is therefore not limited to the psychic realm and can instead offer us a way to measure all things in the universe. I don't believe Buchanan received the warm reception his idea deserved.

Not an advocate of Buchanan's work, Robert Todd Carroll called psychometry a pseudoscience, and it wasn't until 1989 when Leonard

Zusne and Warren H. Jones wrote *Anomalistic Psychology: A Study of Magical Thinking*, which methodically discusses the miracles of human consciousness and behaviors as violating the laws of nature, a notion that is now being proven by researchers in other fields.

In an effort to shift the attention of post- and present-day cynics, I can only draw from an intimate wellspring of information; my own innate understanding that lives within the cells of my body (my firsthand experiences) and scientific sleuths in the fields of physics, cosmology, and molecular biology.

Over the many adolescent and adult years of my life, I questioned the universe and how it works. I never felt quite settled with the word *psychic* and I can recall how people responded to me when I shared my premonitions and spiritual insights. But my questioning mind prevailed, making way for the universe to respond by awakening me to others who were also moved by unseen forces. Albert Einstein tried to construct a theory that could explain all the laws of nature, starting with the tiniest atom and on to the largest galaxy. He used the constancy of the speed of light in James Clerk Maxwell's classical unified field theory in 1905 to unify the concept of space and time.

The notion of there being a connection between scientific theories; theories based on the works of Einstein, Sir Isaac Newton, Charles Darwin, Peter Freund, Herman von Helmholtz, G. Feinberg, C.N. Yang and R.L. Mills, S.W. Hawking, Werner, and Birgit Loewenstein, Michio Kaku, (among other credible scientists); and psychic experiences steeped in intuition and extrasensory abilities has never seemed ridiculous to me. Any attempt to disprove such seemed pointless because all things are made of atoms, which are the basic building blocks of ordinary matter, and matter is anything that can be touched physically. Everything in the universe is made of matter and matter are microscopic books of DNA, having the history of the humble beginnings of all things.

Then, there is energy. What is that made of?

Physicists found that atoms were made up of vortices of energy that are constantly spinning and vibrating, radiating with their own unique energy signature. All things have their own signature, meaning that no two can ever truly be considered alike. Just like fingerprints or snowflakes, no two are identical. We **are** beings of energy and vibration, radiating our own unique signature. Energy, in this regard, is the measure of matter's motion, although it has its own energetic signature.

When using psychometric techniques to measure the energies of a person or thing, our sensory body is reading or decoding the spinning, vibrating, radiating energy signatures to understand the energy we've encountered. Where did that thing come from? What history is held within its atomic structure? What does it like or dislike? What other connections does it have? These questions can be answered by allowing oneself to remain open to the transference and cellular communication that occurs when we use the sensation of touch to unravel or decipher energy signatures. Sound confusing? Don't let it be. Just read and release. Then, consider that you have heard a bit about quantum entanglement. It's another field of scientific investigation, which suggests that two electrons will vibrate in unison when they are close together. Then when separated, they are connected by an invisible thread or, rather, an umbilical cord appears between them, even if they are separated by many light years. Physics calls this the *Einstein-Rosen Bridge*.

When an electron is jiggled, the other electron instantaneously senses the vibration and responds. Physicists call the influencing of electrons at a distance *entanglement*. By merely thinking of someone or something, our thought is composed of electrons.

As a demonstration of the power of one electron within the process of thought, let's imagine an electron, that looks like a Pac-Man figurine, in one biomolecule. It hops on over to another Pac-Man-like figure, an electron-filled biomolecule, and they begin to communicate. That entanglement allows for the transference of information across a seemingly forbidden gap. The action of this transference is known as *quantum tunneling*. A dancing or jiggling electron can be a tangible object, and at the same time, be an oscillation of energy, to be experienced in all realms of consciousness and for all time.

Quantum mechanics holds that any given particle has a chance of being in a full range of locations and...occupies all those places at once. Physicists describe quantum reality in an equation they call the wave function, which reflects all the potential ways a system can evolve. Until a scientist measures the system, a particle exists in its multitude of locations. But at the time of measurement, the particle must choose just a single spot. At that point, the probability narrows to a single outcome and the wave function collapses, sending ripples of certainty through space-time. Imposing certainty on one particle could alter the characteristics of any others it has been connected with, even if those particles are light-years away.

In the quantum realm, events unfold at speeds that would be un-achievable with classical physics alone, as touted by author Mark Anderson in the February 2009 issue of *Discover, Science for the Curious*. He suggests that quantum phenomena are more so seen in laboratory settings, in vacuum chambers chilled to near absolute zero, while biological systems are more notably warm and wet, filled with life noise that could potentially "drown out any quantum weirdness that could rear its head."

While I work on a client, intuitively, I often find it necessary to discount or release the idea of time as I begin to project myself into a person, place, or thing to extract information. The noise or weirdness is part of normal, everyday life. Think for a moment about all the things that distract you during the day. When I tap into you, they will distract me, too. It's also fair to say that it is not an unusual practice to discount up to a third of the data that surfaces while I am trying to harvest true and valid information connected to a specific client.

How does this work in the real world?

If it's true that thought moves at a speed in excess of the speed of light, then information can be sent from the mind of one person to another at breakneck speeds, with little or no effort. We can even think about something; let us use the racecar incident as an example. All electrons associated with that racecar can, in effect, transfer information by quantum tunneling as previously described.

I can't even say that I know or even totally understand everything there is to know about these occurrences. I am merely pulling all the puzzle pieces together to show you that there is an underlying method and powerful force at work in and around our lives. If we take time to understand just how complex we are, we can dispel any mysticism associated with abilities such as mine and realize that we can all perform acts such as these.

It's exciting to think about being a part of an elite club of extraordinary individuals who experience life in profound ways, but the facts speak for themselves. These scientists have documented how the quantum world works; I just don't know whether they realize to what degree our vibrating bodies of energy can influence our environments.

I consider myself to be a grounded serial entrepreneur and seeker of truth. I deal with life like most others, with normal day-to-day human constructs. Yet, I think of something, or touch something, and information is transferred from whatever it is I am focusing on and into the cells of my body to decipher. When working on a client that has body issues and an organ or system is out of balance, vibrating or oscillating at a rate that is not healthy for that individual, my body realizes the imbalance and allows me to feel exactly what the individual is feeling. Then, my inner sight kicks in, allowing me to *SEE* it, as if I am taking a virtual tour through their inner spaces. And seeing it also means experiencing how it's functioning, or not functioning properly.

During the early years of intuitive development, I learned about psychometry from a meditation coach who I had met in Florida. She told me that I could use this technique to extract information about anything by merely placing my hands on whatever I wanted to see into. I could hold someone's keys, a watch, or a ring between my hands and I would be able to pick up information about any aspect of the object or that individual's life. The technique that I was taught was simple and didn't require any force on my part. I didn't have to think per se; all I had to do was be a willing and open conduit for the energy within the person, animal, or object to come through me. By doing so, I was able to feel what they felt, see the world through their eyes, and feel pressure and forces acting upon their physical, mental, and emotional body, thus sensing the energy in and around their body organs.

Psychometry stimulated an area of my brain that I did not know existed, and it incited a new level of understanding within me, revealing just how connected we are to all things made of the same things we are. Atoms, mass, and more.

As I learned more about the process, there appeared to be many uses for this skill set, so I jumped at every chance I got to touch and extract information from whatever I could get my hands on. Touching a tree made me feel as if bugs were crawling all over me, and when the wind was blowing, I felt as if I was swaying in the exact same way the tree was. Touch a dog and I could see through its eyes, see what it saw, who it liked, didn't like, how it ate, where it liked to go, and so on. I could touch a newly trained yearling colt and watch it win its first professional horse race. Touch a human, see through layers of flesh and bone; feel their sorrows and joys. Touch a racecar and, well, you get my point. There seemed to be no end to what I could look at or see into by using the technique. As amazing as it felt, I just had to know how I was able to experience these things. It wasn't enough to just say that I was psychic or intuitive. I had to know that there was a scientific basis for such abilities so that other people wouldn't be afraid of it. With this information, they too could realize their own power.

***

While still dabbling in the racing industry in my late twenties, it became necessary to hire an attorney to help me protect a patent on which I was working. Unbeknownst to us both, something more significant was getting ready to unfold, which came to pass after my attorney's son continued to experience severe vomiting episodes following surgery to repair his esophagus after birth. After much care and medical assistance, the issue showed no signs of letting up. They and their physician were at an impasse, as there seemed to be no workable solutions in sight.

One fateful afternoon, Michael and I met to discuss the patent. He shared their ordeal with their son, saying that they were worn out and feeling quite defeated. He and his wife felt that their hands were tied, and he was worried his son might die. Feeling his fear, I offered to help. I was sure to preface my offer by saying that I wasn't sure what would come of it, but that I was willing to try. I had only spent my time playing with animals and racecars, so working on people would be a somewhat new endeavor.

He accepted my offer, and I met him and his wife on a Sunday at their home. I suggested that he hold his son on his lap to help him feel safe since he did not know me then I placed my right hand on his chest and my left hand on his back. I closed my eyes and relaxed. I almost immediately felt pressure building within my gut, and my stomach became uneasy as if I were going to vomit. I watched the scene unfold as the acid moved up and out of the little guy's gut, burning his esophagus. My body took on his physical mannerisms, as well as his emotional state; I felt listless and scared as the pressure built in my abdomen just before an explosive-like feeling gripped my chest. I watched as the cells of the boy's body showed me event after event where the blood and stomach acid flooded upward and out of his body. Other fluids and food particles not passable via the mouth found an alternate route out of the body by running through the digestive tract and out through the anus. As that scene faded within my mind's eye, I found myself transported to a more specific area of his body. There I was, standing upon the boys' diaphragm, just above a hiatal hernia, looking up into the esophageal tube. The tissue looked soft but red and inflamed. I kept trying to look down toward the stomach, but something kept nudging me to look back up into the esophagus. As I watched, a complex web of veins appeared and then all but one disappeared. The one that remained began to fill with blood like a balloon being filled with water. The ballooning vein reached max capacity and a tear or fissure formed in the esophageal wall, allowing the hot, bloody liquid to pour down past where I stood on the boys' diaphragm, mesmerized by the experience. As I sat with my hands on the lad, I held one question in my mind, *What triggered the event?* As if hearing my thoughts, his body answered my question by showing me that the events were brought on by what the boy had been ingesting. Whatever it was, was continually irritating and inflaming the tissue, exacerbating the situation. Once done viewing what his body wanted to show me, I asked for permission to share the experience with a close friend and medical professional.

My friend and I documented what transpired, illustrating on paper what the boy was going through in a way that the child's doctor could understand. We and the Burgners met for dinner to go over the information, which they then shared with their family doctor. Based on our findings, the boys' physician pulled all medications. The father told me months later that his son vomited once more a week after his doctor pulled his meds. They had been on a cruise and Kaden was eating whatever he wanted, which could have contributed to the last episode, then all bloody episodes ceased.

That experience provoked excitement. It felt good to help people, and by doing so, amazing events such as those I have described made me feel hopeful that there was a divine order or reason for my being alive and awakened to such gifts. I was enjoying my experiences, although there seemed to be no natural flow or order to them. It was so exciting to *see* this way, but I overworked myself to the point of exhaustion. So much so that other people in my life were worried I might burn myself out. As I considered their concern, I realized that there was a need to be more aware and purposeful with my abilities. If I were better able to channel my energy, I might be able to determine the source of the omnipotent energy that was at work in my life and truly know my life purpose. If I was granted this gift to be of service, then there had to be a way to use it without burning myself out.

As I contemplated how to best use my energy, I also had to consider how I had used my energy up to this point, which initiated this next event.

***

My husband and I had started a lawn care service when we first met. After a few years of drought, we were finally blessed with a series of rainy days, which put us behind with our clients by two weeks. My husband was working at the police department at that time, so I decided to load the equipment and set about the task of completing fifty yards, a virtually impossible task for one person to do, as I could only ever manage to get fourteen done on a good day. Realizing that I would push myself to do more than I was previously able to complete, I decided to treat myself to a chai tea as motivation to go above and beyond my past performances. As I pulled through a local Starbucks to make my purchase, I awakened to a new realization. I spent a fair amount of time fixated on the things *I thought* I had to do each day. Not once had I ever prayed for direction or asked the universe whether there was anything I could do to assist in the higher order of life. As that thought filled my head, a new, more peaceful feeling entered my body. It felt as if my brain was expanding, triggering a portal to open at the top of my head that connected me to all life and the universe.

As I relished in the newfound sensation, I noticed something else. Something or someone was in the vehicle with me, although I couldn't see anyone. As if my voice were not my own, I spoke aloud in a way that felt foreign: "I spend each day thinking I know best. I know I've got over fifty yards to do today, but for once, I would like to see a higher power at work in my life. What can I do for you today?" I asked this of the invisible force that was there in the truck with me. Words that were not my own filled my head, offering specific instructions that I was to follow. It happened so quickly: "Drive 9 miles North on Route 29. There, you will find a white car on the side of the road. Stop to speak to the woman in the car."

I couldn't ignore what I had heard. I asked for directions and received an immediate answer. I had never experienced anything like it before. Knowing my day was my own, I decided to follow the directions provided. I would get done whatever jobs I was capable of after I did what I was told. I set the trip meter, as if challenging the information I was given and heard a distinct chuckle.

Imagine my surprise when I crested the top of the hill just before the nine-mile mark and saw a white car sitting on the roadside. I pulled behind the car and noticed a woman leaning into the back fastening her children into their seats. Not really knowing what to say, I stepped out of the truck onto the running board and waved to her. She leaned out of her car to address me.

"Hello, are you okay? Can I help you with something?" I asked.

"No, thank you. My sister had just dropped us back off to my vehicle after a short shopping trip and I was just getting the kids settled so that we could head to the house."

"You're parked in a bad spot on a busy road," I noted. "I am happy to wait until you get the kids ready."

"That is extremely sweet of you, but I'm almost done. I really appreciate you stopping. People don't do this anymore," she said with a heartfelt smile. "You can go on. We'll be fine."

"Are you sure?"

"Yes. Thank you."

I got back into the truck, and just as I began to pull away, I noticed that she was sobbing. She waved at me to stop. I put the truck in park and stepped back out onto the running board. "Yes, is something wrong?"

"I am not sure why I am telling you this but, this morning while praying, I asked God to show me how much He loves me. I just realized that you brought me my answer."

With tears in my eyes, I whispered, "Yes, and you have no idea just how much." I waved goodbye and pulled away. I didn't know how to tell her what had just happened. What took me out of my way, away from starting my lawn care jobs, to have this brief encounter with her?

These instances and many more fueled a fire within me. I had to know how I was able to do these things. I started by looking up the word *psychic* in the dictionary, which implied that experiences such as these would be considered outside the sphere of scientific knowledge and the human mind. That people with such abilities were sensitive to supernatural forces that could not be explained. That was not good enough for me, and I had to know more. I have always felt that I was born with these abilities, as we all are. So, what makes one person use them and not others? Why don't we all tap into these powers? Do we have to possess the desire to tap into such skills? Do we need to be taught to use them?

Understanding the Science: Validating Intuition

Chapter Nine

What Does Science Say About Intuition?

Intuition helps scientists reveal where expertise resides within the brain.

Scientific American posted a study in May 2015 conducted by Kelji Tanaka of RIKEN Brain Science Institute outside Tokyo, where a group of neuroscientists studied the brains of Shogi players using functional MRI (fMRI) to detect the neural signatures of intuitive adeptness within each player. Shogi engages players to use a nine-by-nine board and with two sets of twenty distinct game pieces that face each other. Although like chess, its Japanese counterpart is much more complex. The object is to capture the opponent's king as its players move pieces around a game board. As pieces are captured, they can be dropped "into an empty position anywhere on the board at the discretion of its capturer." As participants engaged in the gameplay, a group of cognitive neuroscientists searched for neural signatures within the basal ganglia of the brain; more specifically, they were drawn to a small region in front of the caudate nucleus, which lies under the cortex.

The basal ganglia receives measured input from the cortex; the outer, rind-like surface of the brain. These structures project back to the cortex creating a series of cortical-basal ganglia loops. This area of the cortex is responsible for the conscious and deliberate analysis of any situation and is associated with conscious perception, whether that perception is familiar to us or unique in nature. The study determined that the caudate nucleus turned on in professional players, while the same region of the brain within amateur players was not as reliable. They went on to proclaim that this specialized area of the brain was less predominantly activated when subjects needed more time to think their moves through, which is a key factor as amateurs choose to engage in developing their intuitive muscle, so to speak. When subjects had up to 8 seconds to search for the best solution, the subcortical region remained silent. As players became more familiar with the rules, they became highly proficient at playing the game, allowing for the pronounced development of the caudate nucleus. The more the players learned, the more superior the signal became.

Their findings tie intuition with the interlinking brain areas called the basal ganglia, which is responsible for learning, as well as executing habits and automatic behaviors. Dr. Watson touches on this area of the brain in her book titled *FLASH, The Science of Intuition*, although she did not directly refer to the caudate nucleus (CN) within the Cortex of the Basal Ganglia, which is where the highly-specialized expert, the intuitive genius within each of us resides. When this area of the brain is activated, the blood flow in front of the caudate nucleus changes and the strength of the CN signal increases, revealing that the subject's brain and intuitive processes studied during Shogi gameplay improved over time. This allowed the players to provide rapid, accurate answers as they learned more about the game. The more the subjects learned, the larger the signal within the brain became.

With repeat practice, the intuitive genius within the brain gets exercised, becoming more sophisticated and precise. Just think, as we choose a specific field of study and fully immerse ourselves into it, the caudate nucleus gets exercised, strengthening a muscle and our intuitive genius takes over. To give a few examples, consider the amount of time it takes for a medical student to become a doctor, and that after 10 or more years of training, a trained physician is able to look at their patient and intuitively know exactly what's wrong with them, only after a cursory scan. Or a skilled art teacher finds an old painting under a pile of rubbish at an estate sale that possesses the signature of a famous artist inscribed on the lower right-hand corner. By looking at the brushstrokes, the teacher intuitively knows that the painting is a fake. Imagine further that with no real training, only possessing a deep love for horses, you're passing a racehorse stable just before the big race. You become mesmerized by a mare that takes your breath away, making your heart race and your hair stand on the nape of your neck. You feel her energy and you know beyond a shadow of a doubt that you are looking at a winner.

When the brain is exercised properly, (like the police officer who trained his brain to pull his firearm in times of danger), we learn to trust what we sense, which allows us to make spontaneous decisions in the blink of an eye, without needing to perform a more thorough analysis. Intuition can be defined as *influence* from the body or brain emerging first as instinctive feelings or sensations. Sounds straightforward, right?

On May 20, 2016, author Cari Nierenberg, a *Live Science* contributor, declared that researchers have found evidence that people using intuition "make faster, more accurate and confident decisions", findings that have been published online in the *Journal of Psychological Science*. Joel Pearson, associate professor of psychology at the University of New South Wales, Australia suggests that intuition does in fact exist, and researchers are now better able to measure it.

Chapter Ten

Energy

F or quite some time, I have hypothesized that energy, mass, and matter have been responsible for universal/sensory forms of communication. The idea has been and is being studied at length by researchers within the scientific communities around the world. Famous men and women of the past and present that I had mentioned earlier have shared their life work, vivifying the origin of the universe, life, energy, mass, matter, our microscopic world, cell theory, cell communication, space, time, dimensions, mathematics, information theory, molecular biology, gravity, the theory of relativity, atomic structure, neurons, quarks, ion channels, quantum theory, electromagnetic radiation, and beyond.

Niels Bohr, a Danish physicist, said, "If quantum mechanics hasn't profoundly shocked you, you haven't understood it yet. Everything we call real is made of things that cannot be regarded as real."

Separate research into each of these fields could be considered a microscopic section of a larger puzzle, yet together, they substantiate the existence of the power that vibrates and lives within all things that are on this planet, as well as out into the multiverses.

Let's look at some of these puzzle pieces. When the puzzle pieces lay apart from one another, some dead ends exist and even nullify one or more of the others, but collectively, as the pieces fit into their respective place, our successes multiply.

The human brain, body, and consciousness have developed over hundreds of thousands of years, and we will continue to evolve because our environments require us to do so. As our environment deviates from past known patterns, our bodies and energy must change to survive and thrive.

Chapter Eleven

Science and Information Theory

W hen I am working with a client, I cannot just stop to look at the physical manifestation of symptoms; instead, I have to consider the physical, mental, emotional, spiritual, and chemical composition to get a clear picture of the balance or imbalance that lies within. I look at the client holistically. We are not flat, like stick figures drawn onto a piece of paper. We are complex, multidimensional creatures, and it is imperative that we view the whole being and treat all aspects of each being with the same degree of respect and attention. In the physical sense, it was important that I learn more about the cells of the body, and that instruction came from the fields of biology, anatomy, and physiology. I knew that living things were not stick-like figures, although I had no idea just how complex and collaborative the cells of the body were until I began my studies. Then came my own ordeals with health and illness coupled with an inner insistence to listen more deeply to the cellular communication between my organs collectively. I often endured the reliving of some horrific experiences or memories that were stored within my cells, where the emotional dimension of my being generated a state of physical disease, all in an effort to help me understand the importance of each dimensional aspect of the self and how *it* responds to life. All things are connected.

The journeys through the cellular realm initiated the next phase of my learning, which provoked the most amazing quest into atoms, particles, mass, matter, energy communication, and the living universe. My body and mind urged me to see the real truth about life and the universal law of "**as within, so without.**" This law states that the outside world reflects what is going on within us, although I would like to take it one step further. Based on my experiences, I have to say that the cells within us are able to communicate at levels that our conscious mind need not be fully aware of. Then, add in all things, or forces, outside us that act upon the body, but which are also in constant communication *with* the body. I mentioned a dance earlier. Imagine now that our environment and body are very much like a great symphony orchestra that consists of musical instruments, performers, and a conductor who collectively compose beautiful music. The music is an arrangement of sounds that in turn produces an effect. In the same sense, the cellular body acts in concert with the particles that make up our environment to produce vibrations, energy, and flow. Each is reliant upon the other and each cannot exist without the other.

I had no doubt that if I followed my gut instincts, I would find the truth and prove that psychic abilities and intuition were not some mystical experience that few could experience. Holding such intentions, my expedition to examine the puzzle pieces accelerated.

As I held the intention to find the truth, the universe reminded me that I was already aware that the pieces existed, that scientists had already done the hard work and all I had to do was connect the dots: Darwin's theory of evolution and natural selection, string theory, Einstein's theory of evolution, gravity, Sir Isaac Newton's Principia formulating the laws of motion and universal gravitation, quantum theory, information theory, the laws of thermodynamics, black holes and time warps, tachyons, quarks, massless extremals, the EPR paradox, FTL travel, wormholes, blindsight, and more.

In each of the above-referenced, famous and not-so-famous scientists conducted research to share how atoms, mass, matter, and energy work together (entangle) collectively in the forming of our universe, the world, consciousness, and our bodies. From The Big Bang through to modern-day quantum theory, it all boils down to energy communication, or for these purposes, information theory, which is measured by entropy, temperature, pressure, or composition, all means by which energy can be measured. But don't take my word for it. Let's look at some of these puzzle pieces. We can start at the beginning with The Big Bang.

"The Big Bang is the dominant cosmological model depicting the expansion of the universe "from the earliest known periods through to our subsequent large-scale evolution...expanding from a very high density and high-temperature state...explaining a broad range of phenomena, including the abundance of light particles, cosmic microwave background and large scale structure which can be attributed to the formation of subatomic particles and later into simple atoms after the particles were allowed to cool."   Britanica.com

Darwin's theory of evolution and natural selection is one of the best-substantiated theories in the history of science. In 1859, Charles Darwin revealed in his book, *On the Origin of Species*, the process by which organisms change over time as a result of changes in inherited physical or behavioral traits. Those changes allow an organism to better adapt to its environment to survive and allow for the perpetuation of life. Quite simply, his two main theoretical points suggest that all life is connected and related to each other and that the diversity of life is a product of "modification of populations by natural selection where some traits were favored over others," favoring "descent with modification" and "survival of the fittest."

Bursting into the physics scene in 1905 is the most influential physicist of the twentieth century, Albert Einstein, sharing his theory of special relativity and educating the world on the underlying unity of matter, energy, light, and time. With that came his theories about general relativity, the bending of light by gravity, the unity of gravity and acceleration, of space and time, and of matter and space. During his work in particle physics, he described the entities that hold together all organizations within the universe and the relationship between particles, the fundamental forces of nature in the unified field theory. These four forces burst forth one by one at the instant of The Big Bang consisting of gravitational force, electromagnetic force, weak nuclear force, and strong nuclear force. At the moment of The Big Bang, all energy and matter were pushed through one singular point called *an unum*, where the density and curvature of space and time became infinite, as portrayed by Hawking and Penrose. This was recorded as the origin of the information. Within each of the four forces resides two of the four forces of nature (strong and weak nuclear forces). The theory of unity sought to inspire the modern quest for the theory of everything. That quest is nearing completion today in the form of so-called superstring, or the unified field theory.

How does the force of gravity affect human consciousness and sensory abilities?

In an article written by *NASA Science, Share the Science* in August 2001 titled, "Gravity Hurts (So Good)", NASA states that "gravity is not just a force, it's a signal." It tells the body how it is supposed to act, how strong the muscles need to be to fight gravity or remain in a certain posture, and more. Blood also feels gravity, as does every system, organ, cell, and organelle within the body. There are sensory receptors within and throughout living organisms that help them learn about any environment they encounter, and it has an uncanny ability to adjust that internal environment at will, not our conscious will, *its* inherent will. When the sensory body picks up a stimulus that can come from various sources, the stimuli are received and changed into electrochemical signals within the nervous system, which changes the cell membrane potential of a sensory neuron.

"The stimulus causes the sensory cell to produce an action potential that is relayed into the central nervous system (CNS), where it is integrated with other sensory information, or sometimes higher cognitive functions, to become a conscious perception of that stimulus. The central integration may then lead to a motor response."

All forces act upon the body and register a sensation. The brain, as do all sensory cells, absorbs and deciphers the sensations, and our bodily cells often react to any and all sensations.

The study of matter in a theoretical world led topologists to determine that matter is changeable, and particles possess the ability to mimic the motion or action of the other. This means *all* matter. To sum this up, everything about life is energy and all energy communicates and acts upon matter. We feel and experience all things, animals, and plants, just as all living things feel and experience, as well. This leads me to information theory, which is the mathematical study of the coding of information in the form of sequences of symbols, impulses, and so on, and how rapidly that information can be transmitted.

In a scientific example, MIT students Aftab, Cheung, Kim, Thakkar, and Yeddanapudi authored a paper titled, "Information Theory, Information Theory and the Digital Age." Their paper offers ideas on how the evolution of a message is handled, its process of waveform transmission, and how it is received. Although this academic paper is related to technology and the transmission of messages, my desire is for you to realize that such processes also occur within the human body and brain, and all living things work much the same way. However silly this might sound, everything about energy and matter sends and receives information in a similar fashion. A living organism is like a supercomputer that communicates with all other energy. Insert the feeling and/or sensation piece and *shazam*, you have a magical work of art that makes life even more complex and exciting.

Let's take a gander down the rabbit hole and see what quantum theory tells us. You may have also heard it described as either the *multiverse theory* or the *many-worlds theory*.

Max Planck revealed it as early as the 1900s and later validated by Einstein that, *"as soon as a potential exists for any object to be in any state, the universe of that object transmutes into a series of parallel universes equal to the number of possible states in which that object can exist, with each universe containing a unique single possible state of that object. Furthermore, there is a mechanism for interaction between these universes that somehow permits all states to be accessible in some way and for all states to be affected in some manner." (TechTarget ~ Whatis.com)*

How does this translate into a real-world experience?

Chapter Twelve

The Language of Energy

While living in New Jersey in my later teens, I worked for a family friend who owned a complete gardening business. One afternoon while taking our usual lunch break, my boss and I chose to visit a nearby park along the Delaware River. We perched ourselves on the picnic benches to eat. We quietly surveyed our surroundings, and it was while in this quiet state that the environment offered the most extraordinary experience. I was savoring my well-deserved lunch when my mind began to wander. I thought to myself, *When I think I am speaking to Great Spirit or God, who am I actually conversing with, and what does this look like?* In a language all its own, the wind, trees, rocks, and creatures answered me in concert. With my eyes fixed upon the bigger view, incorporating the entire landscape, the scene broke apart into tiny little pieces that looked like small balls of vibrating, oscillating energy that swirled and danced around me. At first, the balls of energy were close together, and I could still see the landscape clearly. Then, all at once, they spread apart to leave air pockets between them. Just when I thought it was all over, the atoms or balls of energy overtook my body and I too became small sphere-like balls of vibrating, swirling energy, dancing in unison with the trees, rocks, birds, water, earth, picnic benches, and wind. For the first time in my life, I realized that I was not apart from any of these things but instead, was and am a part of everything.

As I sit here rubbing my hands together like a happy child coveting a piece of chocolate, I realize that my favorite part of my work consists of deciphering the language of energy. In my study of physics, I learned that light sets the universe's speed limit, although space and time are the exception, stretching faster than the speed of light. What does that mean for the speed limit of information transfer? Some physicists suggest that thought is faster than the speed of light and that it is measurable. I'm in full agreement. When in conversation with others, I have noticed some things. When I ask a question, the person I am asking thinks of their response as they begin to speak. My body picks up their thoughts as they open their mouth, and my body translates the full measure of their thoughts before they're finished thinking them.

Chapter Thirteen

Information Organisation

As we meander through a day, we aren't typically aware of the energy and information that's streaming around us. We're caught up in our own thoughts, not mindful that everything in our environment has a life of its own. I'll try to explain by using a simple visualization.

Imagine a storm is forming in the distance. Your physical body detects the subtle changes within the environment as pressure and static electricity build. The smell of the air changes. The temperature and humidity fluctuate creating goosebumps under our skin as the Pacinian corpuscles stand erect.

In the opening story, I shared how I opened myself to the life teaming on and around the mountain, to find out if there was something I needed to know that might affect the trek with our grandson. That level of awareness can be attained by intentionally posing my questions and projecting those thoughts out into the environment, then waiting for an answer.

The sensory organs absorb information from a physical stimulus from or within the external environment, while our sensory receptors simultaneously convert the energy into neural impulses that are then sent to the brain. The brain then organizes the information, decoding and translating it into something meaningful.

At a deeper level, all sensory systems are always awake and aware, even when we aren't consciously aware.

Everything around us is alive and cognizant of our thoughts before we are finished thinking them, although there are times when not all information is available at the exact moment we're trying to connect to any available data. To illustrate this notion, here is a more recent experience I had when I wanted information about working hands-on with an unruly one-year-old canine.

In December 2021, my husband and I bought a home in Tennessee. Months prior, I began working on a remote viewing project to assess a Belgian Malinois dog. I think I had done six separate sessions to address each of the clients' concerns as she tried to find trainers to work with him. None of her initial questions involved me actually doing any training with the dog. Through each RV session, tension and pressure within the dog was building. I mind-melded with him to hear his thoughts. Initially, I was able to determine that he was high energy, unpredictable, and desperately needed daily controlled physical activity. After each new trainer's assessment took place, she would hire me to tell her how he was feeling. His attitude sharpened with each encounter he had with others telling him how he was supposed to be, leaving the owner to wonder whether he would be better off being a house dog. Although every session led to his energy showing that he was built for police or military work, his owner wouldn't submit to him living such a stressful lifestyle, with minimal human contact.

I addressed each of her questions, being noticeably clear on what information I was looking for. I asked the questions in a number of ways to be sure I was probing properly. With each question, the dog's highest and greatest good was always of utmost importance. She wanted to know what his life would look and feel like if he lived a sedentary lifestyle and the universe responded with a very emphatic *no*. He would not conform to a sedentary lifestyle, and as he aged, he would hurt someone if his owner didn't make some fundamental changes. That answer upset her, which led to her asking me whether I would assess him in person to see if we could turn him into a service dog for someone with a physical or emotional disability. My body tensed at the thought, which sparked a discussion about creating a strict protocol that would need to be followed if I were to agree to this visit. The dog would need to be muzzled, leashed, and kenneled for at least the first 4-5 days before I would even start working with him. These things were important for our protection as much as they were for his.

The next time we spoke, we set a date for this visit and circled back through the items I mentioned as necessary for everyone's protection. They were now on my schedule to come before Christmas and potentially stay through the holiday.

Three days before they were expected to arrive, I would remote view it to see if there was anything the universe could tell me about what was to occur.

Before bed on December 18th, I asked the universe to show me if there was something I needed to know. Based on past experience, I knew that some answers weren't always available at the time of questioning, so I went to bed. Then, just before waking, I had a dream where I physically felt myself standing near the inside of our front door. I could see a human and a dog approaching me, and as the dog got closer, it lunged, attacking me suddenly. My heart felt like it had stopped beating and my chest hurt as the breath got knocked out of me, which awoke me instantly without finishing the dream.

I tried to shake the dream, but all I could think of was how mortified I was by the thought of a dog attacking without provocation. I had spent my life loving and working with dogs, so the dream painted a horrific picture of something I had never experienced before, and quite frankly, never wanted to experience.

A day later, a friend from North Carolina visited. Noticing that I was in a state of introspection, she asked what was bothering me and suggested we get out in nature to shake it off. As we walked the loop around a nearby park, I told her about my dream, and how deeply it had disturbed me. I was processing the information as I often do, looking at anything and everything it could mean. Symbolically, it could mean I would have an argument with a longstanding friend or a family member, and they could lash out at me. I looked at the shamanic meaning of dog as an animal totem to see whether the attack in the dream had more to do with me, rather than something or someone outside of me. Lastly, I looked at the potential of it being a physical dog attack, but at that moment, I couldn't imagine what kind of dog would do such a thing. I reasoned that there were no dogs in our house or neighborhood that I sensed that kind of energy from, and in that moment, my friend gasped and reached for my arm. She reminded me of the upcoming visit with this client. As each of her words landed in my brain for processing, I lost my breath. I had been so caught up in our move and in processing the dream that I totally blanked about them coming. As I processed the thoughts further, I took a deep breath and decided to shrug it off. My friend noticed.

"What are you going to do, Nik? I'm thinking you should cancel their visit!"

With another deep breath, all I could think of was how deeply this client loved her dog and how she wanted him to have a life. I wanted to believe that there was a better reason for my interactions with the client and dog. I had to trust that God and the universal energies would always protect me as they had in the past. Why would they not do that in this instance?

I answered her. "I don't want to let this client down. She has such a heartfelt connection to this living being I just can't imagine turning them away."

"Even if it means you get hurt or killed by this dog?"

"Yes. Even *if*."

She processed my answer for a few minutes then posed another. "Well, Nik, if you do allow this, is there anything you can do to keep this from being worse than what you saw in the dream?"

"Sure, the client can do what I asked her to do. Muzzle, leash, and kennel the dog, and I will ask that God and all living things conspire with me for protection."

Now...what I know, based on experience and understanding, is that the universe is always working ahead of us, ahead of my pressing thoughts. So, no matter what I thought was to come, it was all being worked on and worked out before anything was to take place. As the client and I were deep in thought about our upcoming visit, the universe was working on the minute details, behind the scenes.

I could feel the static electricity building and made a mental note of what I felt coming from my dog, my husband, and the trees outside our house that day. Every living thing was reaching out to connect to me.

When she pulled up in our driveway, I opened the front door and motioned for my husband to keep an eye on our German Shepherd. The client opened her car door, and walked to the back, letting a bouncing black beauty, full of vim and vigor, free into my world. At that moment, I blanked on any rational thinking. The discussed protocol was left in the lurch as I opened the door to excitedly greet our visitor.

No leash and more importantly, no muzzle.

I felt my skin begin to crawl. Watching how happy he was to run and be the puppy he was, I invited them into the house. Her pup grabbed a few of our dogs' toys and attempted to play with her. She nipped at him, clearly establishing dominance, which he submitted to. My husband made eye contact with me to suggest that I be mindful as I led the client to the spare room where she was to put the dog kennel and their things. The Malinois, clearly happy to be roaming, leaped on the bed, and bounced like a kid high on sugar; it was at that moment I had a vision of innocently backing toward the bed where he could then snap and attack me. It was that vision that alerted me to how dangerously unpredictable his energy was in the remote viewing session months prior to this. I immediately motioned for the client to go get his kennel from the vehicle.

As I led her back to the front door, the Mali lifted his leg and urinated on our new dining room chair, which led to me telling her to take him with her while she fetched the kennel so I could clean up his mess. She moved swiftly out the door, leaving the dog behind. Everything started to move in slow motion. I was standing at the door watching her, with her dog by my left side. He kept trying to push past me to get out of the door, and I made the mistake of telling him *no*. He looked up at me and I felt something in his brain snap. I held my hand out, trying to establish an energy connection without touching him. He looked back to the door and without a physical sign or warning, he leaped straight into the air at my left eye. As if my hand was being moved by someone else, it lifted straight up to protect my eye and face, allowing the dog to bite my knuckles. From behind me, I heard my husband yell, "Let the dog out." I responded with an emphatic *no*, which led to his loud and resounding response, "LET THAT DOG OUT NOW!"

I opened the door and turned to tell my husband that I was going to tell her that we couldn't help her with this dog. I left safety behind with my attitude fixed on the client, clearly forgetting to keep my eye on the dog at the same time. I approached the back of the car and told her that he had just bitten me. Mouth open, breathing in deeply and hollering his name, the Mali-gator was in the air, then in a millisecond, he latched onto my right arm, shredding it.

Fortunately, knowledge from my prior handler training experience with the police dog trainer kicked in. I used my left hand to get hold of his collar and tried to free my right arm. I was losing my balance when I realized I might not live through this experience. Not knowing whether Monty was there, I hollered for him.

"Monty! I can't stop him. I'm sorry but I need your help." I could hear the client screaming at her dog, but her voice was squelched by his anger and need to dominate the situation.

I remember falling across our driveway face first, then feeling myself slip away. I must have blacked out. When I came to, the dog had my husband on his butt on the ground, teeth pinching into his right shoulder. As I got to my feet, the dog released my husband. In one 10-foot leap, he was on my left arm, attempting to pull me to the ground.

I heard his owner call him one last time, telling him that she was leaving. He released me as quickly as he had attacked and headed for the vehicle, where she secured him.

With that story in mind, we can take the logistics of this all and dive into scientific research and evidence. Werner R. Lowenstein, a world-renowned professor of physiology and director of the Cell Physics Laboratory of Columbia University, was best known for his discoveries in cell communication and biological information transfer. His book, *The Touchstone of Life: Molecular Information; Cell Communication and the Foundation of Life* demonstrates how highly ordered cell matter is shaped and organized to perform coordinated functions. Imagine a living organism that can exist and maintain order under unyielding pressures from outside itself. No matter what the external pressure is, the host for such energy transfers is able to recognize its own energy input and output as well as the input and output of all other energies it encounters, whether in mind or in physical form.

"September 2009 the Universe Forum's role as part of NASA's Education Support Network reported a new form of energy may have powered The Big Bang." In physics, a theory is not a guess or hypothesis, but is instead "a mathematical model that allows us to make predictions about how the world behaves." Einstein's theory of gravity describes how matter responds to gravity. In the subatomic realm, quantum theorists make accurate predictions about how matter behaves at a tiny scale of distance, yet the universal mind suggests that quantum theory and the theory of gravity are not complete unless all fields are unified, plugged into the living form that oscillates or vibrates in constant communication.

To better understand the universe and its beginnings, physicists had to depend on string theory for answers, suggesting that space has more than three dimensions in which we move, and a new window to the universe touts our origins to be related to tiny gravitational waves. Why are gravity waves important? Because they are the only undistorted known form of information that can reach us from the instant of The Big Bang itself. The gravitational waves detected proved that Einstein was right.

Excited about the possibilities of the puzzle pieces coming together, I was drawn to dig deeper. Since cells communicate, I hypothesized that atoms must communicate with each other. Einstein called it "spooky action at a distance." Without being anywhere near another particle, one can immediately tell what the other one is doing. Its scientific name is *quantum entanglement.*

To demonstrate the effect, physicists use two "entangled" mechanical oscillators which can be "anything from a pendulum to a watch spring, to a guitar string," in this instance, they call them *vibrating atoms.* The scientists took a pair of atoms and probed one of them. Faster than light, they seemed to telepathically communicate with one another and the vibrating atom that was not being probed acted as if it was, in fact, probed.

Is it far-fetched to think this way?

In September 2003, trilogy author Philip Pullman wrote and published his own machinations about faster-than-light communication in *The Amber Spyglass.* Although just speculation, Pullman fascinated readers, luring them into believing that spies could converse with their commanders by composing messages on a resonator entangled with a receiver that was worlds away. Silly? No.

In the 1970s, Stanford University and militaries around the globe were testing the idea by teaching soldiers to mind-meld with the use of a technique called *remote viewing*. If we look to the year 2016 and advances in technology, along with how technology transfers information, we can see that it's no longer a speculation, but rather a fact. The invention of the internet, the faster-than-light communication between computers and satellites through space provides us with information at the touch of a button. I reiterate: All things are interlinked and in constant communication.

So, how do we perfect this faster-than-light communication? Practice.

I've been in practice using cell communication for over thirty years, and as a fully sentient being, I have to say that it still amazes me when my body feels something that someone else is experiencing. It had taken me years to realize that not all things I feel are coming from inside me. Being an empath and even using mental telepathy to communicate with individuals who are unable to verbalize what they want to convey out loud, makes me more mindful when my body acts up, or acts out when I'm connected to a client. The cells of my body act in the exact way that the clients' cells are acting while we are in session together.

Chapter Fourteen

Cell Communication, Empathy, And Telepathy

To intimately and genuinely know someone, we must walk a thousand miles in their shoes or get under their skin, so to speak. We must feel what they feel, see what they see, and understand why they have chosen a particular life path. To get that close to someone often means that we must be willing to lose ourselves in the process to fully grasp their "involvedness" in the world.

How might we, as humans, take that leap into oneness, or are we already equipped to do that very thing?

Empathy, telepathy, the sensory system, and the history of perception and sensation are key.

It's long been a matter of philosophical investigation as to whether a
human's ability to perceive distinctive features of space was completely
an acquired ability or exclusively innate via genetic factors (by way of
a sensory apparatus). Were we this way while developing inside our
mother's womb? Yes. My research and in-depth communication with
clients often reveals that as a developing fetus within their mother,
they were able to hear her thoughts, see the world through her eyes,
and experience the world based upon her perceptions, as well as its
own developing perception. How I came to this conclusion and confirmation depends on a few factors as discussed below.

Writings dating back to seventeenth-and eighteenth-century
philosophers and nineteenth-century scientists refer to this issue as
empiricism vs. nativism. Descartes, Kant, Mueller, and others proposed the nativist approach, in which they state that perceptual traits
are inborn. The Gestalt school supports a form of the nativist position, suggesting that tendencies and principles that are considered
innate rule the organization of the perceptual world. Hobbes, Hume,
Locke, Berkley, and Helmholtz, all of whom assumed an empiri-
cist approach, suggest that perception occurs through the learning
processes, through exchange and familiarity with the environment or,
as they put it, "through commerce and experience."

This has been both a logical and an experiential disagreement that
has been quite difficult to resolve. Contemporary psychologists state
that some forms of perceptual capacity and mechanisms may be avail-

able after birth, while theory holds that the genesis of perception emphasizes the interaction of innate and learned factors.

In 1965, R. L. Fantz stated, "Perception is innate in the neonate but is largely learned in the adult." Twenty-five years of hands-on consultations with clients confirmed Fantz's statement that clients (through the use of Cellular Memory Therapy techniques) have been able to retrieve memories about events that had transpired while they were in their mother's womb, and also while they moved throughout childhood, of which they are not fully aware of until they focused on retrieving such data from within the body. This sort of therapeutic experience is more typically practiced by adults who are seeking to resolve life or health issues and is classically not fully understood until one reaches maturity when adults are better able to comprehend any prior experiences that came to mind during therapy.

Chapter Fifteen

Development and Research

I t has been documented that the sensory system of a newborn is well-developed soon after twenty-four weeks of fetal life by way of identifiable eye movement and blink-startle responses that begin prior to birth. Higher levels of visual system structures undergo a rapid rate of development, suggesting that a reasonable level of maturity in anatomy occurs by six to eight weeks of age.

The development of the visual system is more sensitive to environmental influences. During an animal's infancy (the rods and cones), the development of sensory structures and perceptual processes, such as monocular and binocular vision, are susceptible to change and can be irreversibly affected by restrictive or abnormal experiences, also applying to the cortical neurons and neural connections.

If a human were to be raised in a situation where they were deprived of a specific kind of stimulus, what would happen to the cortical cells of an infant, should they be raised by complex interactions of genetic and experiential factors? The authors provided an example of a kitten whose development was purposefully disrupted to see what would happen. The kitten's cortical cells that normally react to visual movement indicating neural responses were disrupted because of extended duration of disuse due to restricted visual stimulation. I propose this example to postulate that human cortical cells would also be disrupted if there were extended periods of disuse, and further suggest that infants not taught to exercise the innate faculties of empathy or telepathy (or other sentient abilities) would have difficulty realizing their true potential unless trained to use them. Most parents don't know how to do that because their parents or friends may not have taught them.

At seven years old, a girlfriend taught me how to read minds, just as her mother taught her. Yet, neither my mother nor my father ever taught me such things.

Research suggests that selective deprivation may cause defective growth or development of neurons in visual pathways and the visual cortex.

Animals raised with one eye receiving more experience than the other become severely restricted, suggesting that an imbalance in the duration of stimulation may cause a "subsequent selective suppression of a portion of the input from the less experienced eye." Many cortical neurons that are naturally sensitive to the absent orientations during rearing become non-functional or unresponsive, thereby losing their orientation selectively.

Exposure to specific orientations becomes necessary to maintain and sharpen the innate response pattern for a given impulse-conducting cell within the cerebral cortex; whereas neurons deprived of activity become silent or non-functioning.

It's then reasonable to deduce that if a child were raised by parents who fostered the child's inherent awareness and encouraged the development of the sensory system outside normal parameters (e.g., normal vision, auditory, feeling, smelling, tasting, etc.), then the neurons would be more fully functional and responsive. Exposure becomes the fundamental influence that allows us to sharpen our perception and innate responses.

I'll complete this section by reinforcing the thought that although my parents had not purposefully participated in or influenced my sensory development, there were key individuals throughout my life who challenged me and helped nurture the innate abilities I use today in my practice. Be mindful that it's not always the parents' task to train their children this way. Life training often comes from outsiders—gifted individuals from outside the family unit.

Chapter Sixteen

Perception of the Newborn Human

I t's been proposed that the newborns of many species of animals recognize a substantial amount of their environment with little or no experience. Something within the cells, within the genetic coding, is the guiding force.

Empiricists consider that a newborn sees nothing more than an "undifferentiated blur," but findings indicate that a newborn can respond to the perceptual world three minutes after birth.

There's importance within studies, such as that of placing a newborn on a mother's back and clicking a toy cricket nearest to the right or left ear and noting that the infant responded with eye movements 18 out of 22 times in the direction of the click 10 minutes after the child was born, indicates that some spatial features of stimulation are picked up and capable of guiding behavior.

Armed with this information, would it then be reasonable to suggest that children can be taught to be more empathic or sensitive? Perhaps, but today, it appears that we are in short supply of empathy, quite possibly due to all the stimuli, the lack of know-how, or the lack of parental guidance in this regard. Most one-parent families (or even two-parent families) appear to lack the time needed to help their children develop into fully functioning, fully empathetic beings. If parents, teachers, and mentors collectively shared in the responsibility, our world might be in better shape.

Chapter Seventeen

Stimulation

The energy emanating from our environment provides necessary information for effective stimulation to the sentient organism, forms of which contain particular biological utilities that are recognized as mechanical (including pressure and vibratory force), thermal, chemical, and electromagnetic (including light energy). Each form can act on specialized sense organs and receptors uniquely suited to its reception.

Imagine for a moment that we're walking down the street. We see a friend approaching. That person sees us, and they're thinking about being excited. They then outwardly act in such a way that reveals their excitement about this unexpected meeting. Unbeknownst to them, they're emanating energy from their body out into their environment and toward us. We are not consciously aware of picking up their energetic signal, but on a more subtle level, all our sensory organs have already gathered data from the other person.

Let's further imagine that, upon striking up a conversation with this friend, the idle chatter takes a turn from being an enjoyable conversation to being negative. Essentially, our bodies were feeling good during the part of the conversation that was enjoyable, but when the discussion became increasingly negative, we began to feel ill or uneasy. To our organs, that negative energy makes us feel as if we have been punched in the stomach, lit on fire, or pushed as the pressure builds to the point of causing us to experience an immediate headache.

Chapter Eighteen

Sensory Receptors

E very living thing has the ability to sense. Indiscriminate variations of the sense receptor structures and mechanisms are formed by natural selection to meet the informational needs required and are adequate for our survival. All forms of life interact with their surroundings, extracting information and performing some form of energy exchange. Even the amoeba, the one-celled protozoa, can receive information without specialized receptors. Most of its external surface is responsive to gravity, light, heat, and pressure.

In multi-celled organisms or animals, the demands of interacting with the environment led to the evolution of receptor cells and units. In response to stimulation, there is a shared function of generating neural activity. A clumping together of receptor units forms sense organs of distinct arrangements and functions that are susceptible to countless forms of energy changes within the environment of an organism. (E.g., the eyes, which are specialized to receive and react neutrally to electromagnetic or radiant energy; taste buds, which react to chemical molecules in the mouth; the inner ear, which receives airborne vibrations; the surface of the skin, which responds to thermal changes and mechanical deformations.) Mechanical energy rightly applied as pressure will influence vision and hearing. Specialized sense receptors developed over time to perform survival tasks for each species through discriminatory responses to particular forms of energy, some of which deliver information to the species about its surroundings. The development of sense receptors is dependent upon their environment and what is necessary for their survival (e.g., a snake will have different sensory receptors than a wolf; a turtle will have different sensory receptors than a hawk; a cat will have different sensory receptors than a bat, and so on).

To further elaborate, we can look to the bat with its highly developed and specialized auditory anatomy. It is most active at night and lives within an environment that is quite dark and that would render photoreceptor mechanisms almost useless. Their sensory structures and behaviors are unique and suited to motion in lightless environments. Their auditory structures or extended range of sound reception and emission allows them to navigate and avoid objects in the dark as they find and catch prey. Several types of animals use echolocation, also known as *bio-sonar*, whereby they emit "calls" into the environment and listen for the echoes that return from objects near them. Animals that use echolocation include some mammals and a few birds, but most notably, the Microchiroptera bats and odontocetes and dolphins, shrews, two cave-dwelling bird groups, and more recently, humans. Studies are being conducted that revolve around teaching the blind to see by directing "calls" or energy signatures out into one's environment, and by doing so, they can detect just how close they are to an object.

Now, this leads us to pose the question: Can someone inadvertently detect objects within their environment without intending to do so?

***

One evening, while babysitting for my brother in Spring, Texas, I fell asleep on the couch after putting the kids to bed. I began to wake up but had not yet opened my eyes. Interestingly, with my eyes closed, something happened. The entire room lit up in a field of green; different shades of green that went from light to dark; yet, as I explained, my eyes were closed. In past experiences, the room has lit up in different shades of red, alerting me to negative and tragic experiences that were coming my way. And so, I could only conclude that this green light meant all was well and that the spirits were happy.

Chapter Nineteen

Principles of Echolocation

E cholocation is the same as active sonar, whereby an animal itself emits sounds. The effective operation is done by measuring the time delay between the animal's emitted sound and any echoes that return from the environment.

The relative intensity of sound received at each ear, as well as the time delay between arrival at the two ears, provide information about the horizontal angle from which the reflected sound waves arrive.

The bat's auditory system is adapted to orient them and locate objects. They are dedicated to sensing and interpreting the "calls" typical of their species. This specialized system operates from the inner ear on up to the auditory cortex, which is where the highest level of information processing takes place. Human echolocation can be performed in much the same manner by intentionally sending energy or a specific thought out into the environment to communicate or connect with another human or thing, in an effort to retrieve physical, mental, emotional, and even spiritual information, to find and retrieve objects connected to another human, to communicate parapsychologically allowing one to hear another's thoughts and to empathically feel and understand how another person experiences life. This form of communication is not well known but has been achieved unintentionally by twins, between mothers and their children, and amongst husbands and their wives. Developing our specialized sensory structures increases the potential to extract information from our environment, no matter what environment that might be. As our range of functional demands increases, there is an even greater need to make finer sensory discriminations.

Sensory receptors required to perform such specialized tasks are the brain, eyes, ears, nose, mouth, teeth, skin (being the largest of our sensory organs), fingers, hands, and feet. But we must look deeper than this. C. Norman Shealy, a North American neurosurgeon, writes that the foundation of his interpretation moves beyond that of the physical form to describe the body as having "seven major sheaths and subtle bodies around the physical form quite like that of an energetic envelope. There are higher and lower astral bodies as well as higher and lower mental bodies with an outside astral or emotional body, mental, causal, and spiritual body manifesting in all subtle energy from the physical body outward."

Life experiences impact both our mental beliefs and our physical bodies, which can be empathically and intuitively "understood" by specially trained practitioners. Individuals accustomed to seeing auras can use what they see to decipher colors and energetic signatures within the body as either healthy or unhealthy.

When I am assessing the health of a target (a living, breathing being), I don't just look into its physical organs and how they function; I also look at the energetic or etheric energy outside the physical form.

While working in my garden one summer afternoon, a neighbor walked over to hand me a check for mowing her yard. I sensed that something was wrong. I used my energy to assess hers as she crossed the street. Her aura looked brown and mottled with black swirling dots. I stood to greet her as she handed me the check. I tried to speak to her, but she didn't respond verbally. I asked her if she was okay, and she shook her head. I dropped what I was doing and walked her back home, assessing her energy more deeply. As my body processed the mottled black swirling dots, I felt pulled to look into her lungs. I let myself see, hear, smell, taste, and feel the information that I was receiving.

Communicating with her lung cells, I took note of her oxygen levels, which felt low. I could smell natural gas, which made her heart race, creating an alert response in my body. I stepped into her house and the danger response was confirmed. The whole house wreaked of natural gas. I walked her out into the yard and called the gas company for assistance. The fire department, an ambulance, and the police came quickly to manage the scene and rectify the issue. She was taken to the hospital and released a few days later.

A few days later, I was out walking my dogs just after dark. I passed her house and felt drawn to look at a towering tree in her backyard. Sitting perched high in its limbs were 20 vultures. I connected to them, as a shaman typically does, knowing that all creatures bring us messages. The message vibrated through my body as I felt what she was experiencing. Her health issues were more serious. Not doubting what I felt or heard from the vultures, I called her son that night to alert him. He called me a day or so later to let me know that she had had a heart attack.

Sir William Osler, one of the four founding professors of Johns Hopkins Hospital, points out that there is one cause of any one illness and "if we look for that one cause, we will find that it is the interaction of all factors; physical, mental, emotional, spiritual, chemical, and electromagnetic; that determines the health of the physical form."

Should we agree with Osler on his viewpoint of there being one cause to any one illness? I will let you decide.

***

Jeremy, a twenty-three-year-old male, has experienced uncontrollable vomiting from 2010 to 2014, episodes of which could only be remedied by medical care. Upon our first visit, I placed one hand on his abdomen and one on his back to *see* into his body. As I did so, I held a request in my mind. That request is the same each time I perform this type of task: "Show me," which equates to my asking the body of the client to reveal what, where, when, and how an imbalance had manifested within the body. The cells within Jeremy's body revealed an elevated level of emotional stress connected to the work that he was performing with a family member. If I had stopped at the emotional trigger, I would not have seen what appeared next. The body then shifted from the emotional body into the physical, revealing a network of veins that feed the stomach. One vein near the top section of the stomach appeared to be inflamed. There was a sensation of mild paralysis in the stomach and into the top section of the small intestines, which suggested that each was having difficulty processing food due to a lack of blood flow. His body shared this experience while I watched. As the food passed into the small intestines, it felt as if it was almost paralyzed to a certain degree and, as the food entered, it began to back up quickly, not able to pass. As the food packed into the intestinal space, the processing in the stomach did not halt. The pressure built, and when the stomach could not take any more pressure, the food was catapulted into the esophageal space and out of the mouth. This process repeated itself until the pressure was released. Although the body suggested that the emotional state of the client was the trigger for the illness, I had to also look more deeply at any physical abnormalities that existed before the stressors triggered an involuntary reaction, whereby the body itself finally "showed" signs of distress.

As I evaluated the multiple stresses in Jeremy's life, I was then drawn back into the body to look just above C1, and then further down at C5 and C6 of the cervical spine, as well as T7 and T12 of the thoracic spine, where nerve impulses were being interrupted. His body then communicated that during the birth process, something had transpired that caused a disconnection of energy in his cervical spine. The energy should flow freely through the spine to various organs and systems, but there was a disconnection felt and seen leading into the digestive system. Once this final piece presented itself, I went back to plug in all the variables.

Simply put, Jeremy's body allowed me to feel the stress he was experiencing in his life, but his body showed me that there were physical anomalies connected to the spine and stomach disrupting the digestive system. Can we agree with Osler that there is one cause for any one illness? That may be a matter of perception.

The emotional stress of working for his family, feeling as if he has to prove himself, not eating properly, the body not having the ability to extract nutrients and digest food properly, drinking excessive amounts of alcoholic beverages, and working in the Florida heat in a fixed body position for extended periods of time were all factors that led this body to rebel and show an extreme level of distress. When I shared this with Jeremy and his mother, she shared that he was born with the umbilical cord wrapped around his neck, and Jeremy then stood to reveal the marked malformation of this thoracic spine, which runs from T7 through T12. For our organs and systems to work in harmony, the nerve innervations need to be free of disruptions.

Richard Gerber, medical doctor and author, in his text on vibrational medicine, introduces concepts established during research performed by Harold Saxton Burr. These concepts reveal the existence of electromagnetic fields whereby a template of sorts is generated that regulates the development of health, the disposition of an organism, and its vibratory force. Noting the energetic qualities of various life forms from the 1920s through the 1940s, Burr evaluated the electrical fields of trees during season changes, the cycles of the moon, hormonal changes in women, and malignant tissues, which would allow doctors to detect illness before any accustomed symptoms would occur. His work suggested that "all living things are formed and controlled by electrodynamic fields," which led to the development of what came to be better known as the *L-fields*, used to explain cellular differentiation.

I believe that our bodies, being the "multifaceted cohesive life-energy structure housing the soul and all its creative expressions," through vibration are able to decipher the signals returning from a target of interest, which can be heard, seen, felt, tasted, and smelled in the ultrasonic range, far outside the range of standard human physical sense organs. Note that perception is based upon the environmental stimulation reaching the sense organs.

Chapter Twenty

Human Bio-Sonar Capabilities

J ames T. Fulton discusses the potential for human echolocation by means of which he compares human physiology and linguistics with the highly enhanced structure of the Bottlenose Dolphin, along with other members of the Cetacean family of whales and dolphins, in hopes of training humans to use their sensory body to perform echolocation more effectively and to assist those with vision impairments.

Fulton references an instance where a young blind gentleman is "able to ride a bicycle and traverse familiar territory with extraordinary skill based on the use of his acute hearing and augmented by vocalizations designed to provide echolocation information." As I referenced earlier, I had not only one but two vivid experiences where I had closed my eyes to go to sleep, and while in that relaxed state, my body sent out vibratory signals throughout the room without my conscious effort, which in one instance lit the room up, revealing the many objects in shades of red and in the second instance, revealed many objects in shades of green. To this day, I don't know what provoked the experiences, nor have they recurred since, but the two experiences did incite thoughts about teaching visually impaired children how to see. Using this line of focus, I began to teach (or play games with) my five-year-old grandson to determine whether he could read my mind in an effort to prove that the brain and body can see, hear, smell, and even taste the thoughts of another person.

Our first game began at the dinner table. It helped that he loved to watch me work and was quite intrigued with my abilities. I took a few minutes to explain to him how deep breathing helps to bridge the body and the mind, but also reduces any internal chatter. I then chose five foods that were on the table before him. I told him that I was going to think of only one food item that I would then send in thought to him via a mental image. As I sent the thought and mental image to his body or brain, I asked that he only be receptive to what I was sending and not try to think of what it was on his own. When the image registered in his mind's eye, he was to notify me directly. Interestingly, as the food item appeared in his mind, he got incredibly happy. Each time, he smiled and then shared what that item was. I then offered high praise to anchor in the good feeling around getting it right.

As he got better at playing the first game, I began to open the field up to include all the objects on the table, and I was sure to use the same techniques in visualization that worked during our first game. As he became more comfortable with the added objects, I then opened the field up to include all the objects in the kitchen. When he became more comfortable with that, I then began to include people and animals within the house. Then, I began to think of people, animals, and objects outside the house, and then on to allow for numbers or math to be added, and then on to thinking in sentences rather than trying to send only one word at a time.

The contemplation of such leads me to ruminate on J. J. Gibson and his affordance theory. Gibson, one of the most important twentieth-century psychologists in the field of visual perception, proposed that "animals guide their behavior by perceiving directly what environmental objects or encounters offer or afford for action." As animals obtain data from the outside world, information is picked up through direct perception, not through mental processes. Data is retrieved via the sensory organs identifying a combination of the properties of an object's substance and its surface with reference to its needs, capabilities, and environment, which should be viewed as interlinking. As such, those needs and capabilities cannot be viewed as separate. The term *affordances* is defined as *the affordances of anything is a specific combination of the properties of its substance and its surfaces taken with reference to an animal. The affordances...are the possibilities for action that it offers or provides the organism.*

Gibson emphasized the traditional study of the sense organs, preferring to focus on the information-gathering aspects rather than considering the sense organs as a passive receiver of imposed stimulation. He proposed a classification based on "modes of activity" and on the types of data harvested by the active organism; the organism's behavior being the central focus; looking, smelling, and tasting being accomplished by perceptual systems and the information obtained. An important piece of information within his works revolves around his notion of a haptic system that would include the skin, joints, and muscles, along with sense modalities such as gustation (taste) and olfaction (smell).

Chapter Twenty-One

Echolocation and Telepathy for Search and Rescue

While out walking my dog one morning in Tennessee, I happened upon a man standing at the end of his driveway. Holding a portion of a leash in one hand, his eyes desperately searched the surrounding landscape for something. His energy felt very disturbed, with tinges of extreme sadness mixed in. I stopped to see if I could help. He relayed that he had his two dogs cinched to the leash handle, which he held out for me to view. They each had their own leash; however, they were connected to one central pin. He said the dogs were extremely excited and pulled him down the driveway as if they were hot on the trail of something. The leash broke and it had been an hour since he had seen them rushing off into the mountain underbrush. Taking a moment to survey the area, I noticed we were surrounded by trees, underbrush, and extreme drop-offs. There were houses mixed sparsely into the landscape; however, there was way more uninhabitable land around us. I could empathize with his sadness and fear.

Without voicing his concerns or my own, I asked him if he understood psychic or intuitive abilities. He said he was aware of them; however, he didn't have much experience with them personally. I told him that if he held a picture in his mind of what the dogs looked like and then envisioned himself as a lighthouse—sending his light out to show them the way home—I could use his thoughts and energy to track the two dogs. After a lighthearted laugh, he agreed to give it a try. I talked him through the visualization process and closed my eyes to initiate my bio-sonar/echolocation and telepathic abilities. I turned away from him and followed the energy line that ran from him and out into the mountainous underbrush. My loyal Lab followed me without issue and sure enough, within a quarter mile, his dogs were standing quietly affixed to a fallen tree. Their leashes were tangled in its branches, and the largest of the two dogs diligently chewed at his portion to free himself. I watched for a minute to be sure not to spook them. The dog that was chewing his leash could have gotten free; however, the smaller and more docile dog may have gotten left behind had I not found them.

Chapter Twenty-Two

Mental Telepathy and Signal Detection

E cholocation has come to denote passive and active spatial awareness, primarily referring to aural *imaging* of a nearby environment based on ambient background sound rather than active echolocation, images being "the universal language" no matter what dialect one may speak. It is within Fulton's research of Blesser and Salter's work that we find their comprehensive use of the term *echolocation*, noting that, "sensory skills are acquired, rather than innate; they are based on personal utility and lifestyle."

It has been within my own studies, as well as client-practitioner interactions, that I telepathically communicate while using remote viewing or mind-melding with my targets, but also with those who are not able to verbalize their wants and needs due to illness or injury. To set the stage, I began teaching my grandson telepathic games and then moved from there into using psychometry to peer into organs and systems, but first, I started with the simple games as described in the prior chapter. Although I had used echolocation in business, I had not taught anyone to use my applications for such things.

While teaching my grandson how to read my mind, the echo happened quite by accident. I set the stage to play a game during lunch to be certain he was experiencing the same effect each time. On a piece of paper, I drew eight stick figures, each one being different from the others. Once done drawing, I told him that I was thinking of only one of those figures and I wanted him to do his deep breathing to engage his sensory body. He did as he was told, and when he smiled, I knew he saw the figure in his mind's eye. I would then ask him to tell me what he saw. He informed me that he did not see the figure in his mind, but rather heard an echo bounce off the page as he felt me thinking of it.

Telepathy, also known as thought *transference*, refers to the transmission of information from one person to another without any known sensory channels or physical interactions. I would have to add that the word "known" must correspond to being consciously aware of or paying close attention to the sensory channels while performing such an act. It is my personal opinion, based upon experience, that as multidimensional beings, we may use one, two, or more of our sensory channels during this type of exchange as information is retrieved in symbols and images, type-written words that come to mind, feelings, or emotions.

During studies using the Ganzfeld experiment, in which one individual was designated the sender and the other the receiver, the sender would select a random card and visualize the symbol in an effort to send or transmit the picture to the person receiving the information. Psychical researcher John Arthur Hill describes telepathy as "no physical theory of telepathy...no 'brainwaves' known, and no receiving stations yet discovered inside our skulls." H. H. Price, a well-known philosopher, says that there isn't any material explanation that would reveal radiations detectable on physical instruments.

Parapsychologists describe four forms of telepathy, all of which I have experienced throughout my life: 1) Latent telepathy, whereby one transfers information through Psi (parapsychology) with an observable time-lag between transmission and reception; 2) Retrocognitive, precognitive, and intuitive telepathy, which is the transmission of information about the past, present, or future state of one individual's mind to another; 3) Emotive telepathy, which is also known as remote influencing or emotional transfer, suggesting the process of transferring kinesthetic sensations through an altered state; and 4) Superconscious telepathy, which involves extracting information from another individual.

***

Wayne Carr of the Western Institute for Remote Viewing in Washington State called one day to provide me with a target number for a job he needed me to do. This "target" needed to be found. I was not front-loaded, meaning I was given only the target number that would represent the object of focus and was fed no other information about what this target was. During the remote viewing session, I determined that this "target" was in fact a male who had worked in the military field and was quite dehydrated. As I mind-melded with him, I saw through his eyes. I saw him hunker down in a storm drain-like tunnel on the side of a roadway during a bad thunder and lightning storm and further determined that he was safe. He explained that he had gotten very dehydrated while working, and after work, had gone home to sleep but awoke, wandered out of the house in the wee hours of the morning, and did not know where he was. I saw the days turn to night, signifying that he had been out for a couple of days at least. I saw and heard the planes flying overhead which did not look like commercial airplanes. They looked and sounded more like military planes. He then informed me that he had been picked up by a nice couple who had taken him to a roadside facility to feed him. They also gave him money so he could get back home. Nearing the end of the session, he insisted that he had been found by the police near a military base in southern Texas and that they were on their way home. At this time, I ended the session, called Carr, and then called the family to explain that they all needed to head back to the house because the police were bringing him home. Within one hour, they called me back to confirm that the police had, in fact, brought him home. He was very dehydrated, and his family took him to the hospital for a few days to receive fluids and a more thorough exam. When he got well, his family told him that I had telepathically communicated with him during his travels. He was astounded because he had no recollection of it but confirmed that what I had telepathically retrieved during the session was true.

My belief? Perception is not only available before birth; it can also be learned. My individual experiences as an empath and telepath have provided deep insight into what infants experience while in their mother's womb, but also indicate that children, as well as adults, can tap into their own innate abilities by conscious choice with the aid of a skilled practitioner to assist them in developing their abilities further as they experience connecting with the electromagnetic fields or life force of others.

Chapter Twenty-Three

Cell Communication and Cellular Memory Detoxification Therapy

W e humans are not separate from any other thing and because of this, we are able to communicate with all things within our realm of consciousness. The God-source energy manifested itself on this plane of consciousness through our bodies and has since been in constant communication, aiding us throughout our lives. I think humans are finally ready and capable of understanding and embracing this philosophy.

The Cells, Organs, and Systems

In 1665, Robert Hooke discovered the cell while examining thin slices of bottle cork under a coarse compound microscope. This microscope magnified the cork and allowed him to see a multitude of pores within its structure, which, to Hooke, appeared to have walled compartments that resembled the ones he was familiar with where monks lived. It was because of this association that he decided to name these compartments, *cells*.

The cell is the smallest basic biological structural and functional unit of life, of all known living organisms. Cells have been referred to as the "building blocks of life," which are broken down into four distinct categories by structure and function and are further broken down into four *tissue* types. Tissue is a group of cells that are similar in structure and function, comprised of the epithelial, muscular, nervous, and connective tissues. Comprised of two or more tissue types are the *organs* that execute specific bodily functions. And then we have the organ systems, 11 in all which are a group of organs acting together to accomplish certain bodily functions.

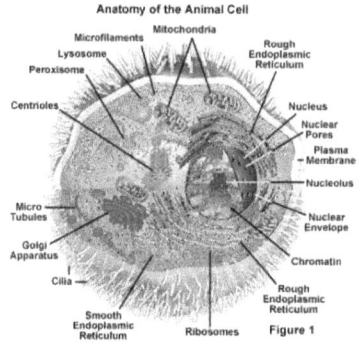

Anatomy of the Animal Cell

Figure 1

Molecular Expressions

Anatomy of the Animal Cell

For example, the organs of the digestive system work together to break down goods moving though the digestive tract and absorb the end products into the bloodstream to provide nutrients and fuel for all the body's cells.

In terms of the elemental composition of the human body, we can examine either mass or atomic composition being comprised of 53% water. It is 11% hydrogen by mass, or 67% hydrogen by atomic percent. Much of the mass of the human form is oxygen, but we must consider that most of the atoms within the body are hydrogen atoms. And so, 99% of the human mass is made up of five elements (oxygen, carbon, hydrogen, calcium, and phosphorus, with only 0.85% being composed of another five elements (potassium, sulfur, sodium, chlorine, and magnesium, along with some remaining trace elements). In terms of molecular type, the body is composed primarily of water, proteins, connective tissue, fats, bones, carbohydrates, and DNA. In tissue typing, the body is broken down into water, fat, muscle, and bone categories, and in cell typing, the body consists of hundreds of diverse cells; the largest number encased within its folds are not human cells but bacteria, which reside within the intestinal tract.

No matter what we choose to focus our energy upon as we assess the body, we must consider, from a conscious vantage point, that we have not had to give thought to the functioning of these systems, parts, or processes for each to do its job. All maintain constant contact, communicating with each other twenty-four hours a day, knowing exactly how to act with or react to, any given environment and/or stimulation from outside itself.

If one thing is out of balance, it may throw off other systems until we consciously catch on and do something about it.

Chapter Twenty-Four

Sensory Abilities and the Cell's Ability to Communicate

For an organism to be able to perceive or be aware of its environment, it must depend upon processes that can detect stimuli and then convert said stimuli into a form that is understandable and able to be processed by the nervous system. Examples of such abilities are cats that can see in the dark, eagles that are able to see mice from extreme heights, and bats and dolphins that have hearing so finely tuned that they can detect signals echoing back to them after their signals have bounced off objects within their environment. As you can see, the sensory system is quite proficient at detecting stimuli. But how does it do it?

Sensory events involve light, heat, chemical, or other energies in the environment, but it has been suggested that our nervous system does not directly identify those events. Each sensory event must be converted into electrochemical nerve impulses to be processed. Another name for this conversion of energy is *transduction*, which is done by each sensory modality via dedicated sensory cells. These cells are not neurons, although they produce electrochemical impulses that the neurons can decode.

Sensory cells involved in the detection of stimuli can be found on the skin: Pacinian, Ruffini's, and Meissner's corpuscles, Merkel's disks, and free nerve endings, which provide various forms of information about pain, pressure, vibration, and tension, while free nerve endings deliver the sensation of cold and heat. The taste buds on our tongue have sensory cells called *chemoreceptors*. There are also different chemoreceptors involved in olfaction, which are found on nerve endings that descend from the brain's olfactory bulb into the sinus mucosa. If sensory cells are not activated by a sensory event in any of these cases, there will be no perception or sensation of that event.

Chapter Twenty-Five

How Cells React to Stimulation

Like animals, humans are capable of emitting sounds or sending signals, which, in turn, will pick up signals and retrieve data from other objects, returning to the sender via echoes from the target environment when focused upon.

While the innate ability in animals may not require their conscious thought, we, humans, need to be more intentional about using the ability to master the techniques, to the point of not having to think about it and to the point where it becomes a natural or automatic response to a thought we hold in our mind. Human echolocation can be performed by intentionally sending one's energy out into the environment to communicate or connect with another human or thing, in an effort to retrieve physical, mental, emotional, and even spiritual information about that object, to find and retrieve objects connected to another human, or to communicate parapsychologically, which allows one to hear another's thoughts, and to empathically feel and understand how another person experiences their life, but even still happens without our conscious will. Developing our specialized sensory structures increases the potential to extract information from our environment, no matter what environment that might be. As our range of functional demands increases, there is an even greater need to make finer sensory discriminations.

Through repeated sessions over twenty years with clients, I have come to understand that physical bodily sensations are codes or distress signals that the cells within our body send out in response to a particular stimulus, such as our thoughts or actions. These sensations are the results of our mental beliefs and the emotions that we experience at the peak of a specific event. If we focus on the one cause or root of an issue rather than the presenting ailment of any one illness, and if we intentionally look for that one cause, we will find that it is the accretion of all factors, physical, mental, emotional, spiritual, chemical, and electromagnetic that will determine the health of the physical form.

As we decipher the signals returning from our target of focus, our sensory cells share information that can be heard, seen, felt, tasted, and smelled in the ultrasonic range, far outside the range of ordinary human physical sense organs.

If we were to begin training at the earliest possible age to familiarize ourselves with our true potential, we could magnify our inherent capabilities to gain a better understanding of how our thoughts, words, and actions affect our sensory cells, organs, and systems.

Animals influence their behaviors by perceiving what environmental objects or encounters make them respond in specific ways. The needs and capabilities of the animal and its environment are studied without separation and, as such, they cannot be viewed as separate. As the animal senses something about its environment, the sensations will trigger sensory cells within the nose, mouth, eyes, and ears, which, in turn, will create associations.

Conventionally in Western cultures, the body was viewed as a "bio-machine" but presently, our focus is being drawn to the "information gathering" aspects of oneself, rather than looking at the sense organs as passive receivers of imposed stimulation. As multidimensional beings, our physical, mental, emotional, and spiritual characteristics are divinely interwoven, creating a matrix that has the capacity to either create or disrupt currents of energy. In either case, our energy extends outward, instigating an effect that impacts our target of focus, or our external environment, either positively or negatively, while our inner environment is being bombarded by the stimulus from the external world.

Chapter Twenty-Six

Everything Communicates

E verything around us and within us is made of energy and mass, which communicates with everything else. I hypothesize that it is our cellular mass that acts as a storage system of sorts, capturing every millisecond of every day. When we get overloaded or stressed, the cells send out signals to tell us that they are unhappy or overloaded, thus requiring our attention to relieve any conflict they may be experiencing. These signals may take the shape of unbridled emotions, appear as nervous-like twitches, or some other involuntary body tick. The imbalance may feel like a pain (sharp, stabbing, chronic, or radiating), manifesting as a particular type of illness (such as Fibromyalgia, chronic fatigue syndrome, bronchitis, post-traumatic stress disorder, Parkinson's disease, or cancer), or it may feel like a minor discomfort (such as mild back pain, facial or eye twitches, nasal congestion, or a headache). If our perception or our sensory cells' perception of an event that transpires triggers these bodily reactions, then any of these imbalances may be strictly emotional in nature, rather than a potentially inflexible physical ailment. An emotional imbalance can signify a time of ripeness within our body, a time in which we can turn inward to communicate with the cells to determine the exact trigger of an imbalance. Within my professional practice, I have worked with individuals who had developed maladies on the physical plane and the cells were still able to restore balance.

Since the cells can communicate with one another to perform intricate functions, it stands to reason that we, being of divine consciousness, have the ability to focus our awareness upon any one thing and extract information that will assist the body in reestablishing homeostasis on its own, without external intervention. It should not matter whether the dysfunction had been lurking within your body for thirty-six years (like Spieth's) or whether you just began experiencing pain or discomfort today.

As I force myself to sit at the computer to write, edit, read, and edit some more, my neck and shoulders ache yet I continue to hold myself to my perceived agenda of getting this book completed. The cells within my head, neck, and shoulders are communicating with each other that this behavior needs to shift, or else! I type on. Hours later, after these cells are exhausted from trying to get my attention to help them rebalance, they give up on trusting me to do the right thing. They realize that they will have to adapt to my poor posture and behavior.

If I give my body the break it deserves, the cells will calm down and get back to performing more important tasks in other parts of the body. When we use our senses to listen to what the body is trying to tell us and drop our perceived agendas, we can then fully realize the cells' innate wisdom. If I had followed my inner guidance and taken a much-needed break, the body would have alleviated the pain and discomfort much quicker. When we listen, systems rebalance, and our breath, inner peace, and trust are restored.

As I unconsciously assess the discomfort, as I have grown accustomed to doing, a question comes to mind. When did I adopt the behavior of pushing myself like this? Not giving myself a break when I need one. Not giving my family or my dog the love and attention they need and deserve. Before the thought is complete in my brain, my cells are already activated, as if they knew exactly what I was thinking before I thought the question through.

In response to my question, a memory surfaces, bringing clear images into my mind's eye. I see myself back in first grade; my teacher is making me sit at my desk to draft an essay as punishment for not having completed it sooner. So, while everyone else went outside to play, I sat hunched over the desk scribbling out a story. As if I were right there with the teacher again, I could hear her say, "Do your work first, then we'll see if there's time for you to play."

When focusing your intention on finding a trigger event, the body will show you which experiences are stored and allow them to surface. Neurons are activated by our thoughts and imaging is initiated. Then, the sensory cells pool to generate sensations that reveal any and all prior experiences. The imagery will show up in the mind's eye much like a daydream, and just like in a daydream, you will feel sensations throughout other parts of your body.

When I work with a client, I purposefully guide them through the questioning process, all the while allowing my body to feel what they are feeling. In most cases I am able to pick up the images of their stored memories and my body will feel their emotions as if I am right there living through it with them. Energy signatures transferred from one person to another are therefore unconsciously assimilated by performing such an act.

Chapter
Twenty-Seven

Cellular Memory

Cellular memory is described as a hypothesis stating that "such things as memories, habits, interests, and tastes may somehow be stored in all the cells of human bodies, not just within the brain." The suggestion is based largely on anecdotal evidence of organ transplants, after which the recipient was reported to have developed new habits or memories.

Specialized fibers that differ in size and speed of transmission carry pain and other information by way of myelinated or unmyelinated fibers; the technical name for pain transmission is *nociception*, which means "the perception of damage or injury." In the aforementioned situation, the damaged tissue releases chemicals that produce substances emitted by the immune cells. Those immune cells then produce allergic reactions (histamines) or substances resembling unsaturated fatty acids that perform a similar function to that of hormones, which control body temperature, inflammation, smooth muscle contractions, and blood pressure (prostaglandin). These chemicals make it easier for stimuli to cause pain fibers to fire within the body when they would normally not do so.

Cellular Memory Detoxification Therapy (CMDT) and its uses

Cellular Memory Detoxification (CMD) is a method or inner balancing practice whereby we communicate with our sensory cells, organs, and systems to free memories and sensations stored within the cells of the body that cause physical, mental, emotional, and spiritual imbalances.

By taking a hands-off approach (or a third-party stance), one can use deep breathing techniques to calm the mind to focus inwardly, forging a connection with the sensory cells to communicate and gain access to information stored within any organ or system. Once the mind is calm, the inquirer will ask the sensory cells questions and then listen for a response. The inquirer may see images, feel emotions or sensations, hear a voice speaking the answer, or perhaps even see type-written words as if some unknown force is responding to the inquiry.

To communicate with the cells to allow for detoxification and re-balancing, you might imagine having a conversation with your best friend rather than moving to manipulate the conversation by digging for memories that you may or may not remember. This process is not about digging but rather allowing the sensory system, which is responsible for processing sensory information, to show and tell what it has stored within the cells of the body.

Cellular Memory Therapy has been used in the prevention of disease, defeating addictions, lifestyle changes (nutrition, exercise, etc.), in the motivation of athletes and non-athletic individuals, as an aid for healing, recovery from syndromes, ailments, dysfunctions, emotional and behavioral disorder detoxification, pre-surgical, surgical, and post-surgical rehabilitative procedures, analysis of life, healthcare choices, and so much more. Its applications are endless.

CMDT Conclusion

From the top of our head to the plantar aspect of our feet, the afferent and efferent pathways of the spinal cord to the epidermis of the integumentary system, or from the innermost workings of the cell to the energetic body which extends outward away from the physical form, we are sensory.

Chapter Twenty-Eight

Remote Viewing (RV)

History

More than one hundred years ago, scientists began their quest to legitimize claims relating to the presence of sensory perception, perceptual abilities whereby individuals were able to recognize and explain data that was retrieved without going to a specific location, or without being in the same room with a person or thing that needed to be examined. This scientific inquiry began within the field of parapsychology in the United States as well as abroad. Its nature was examined within the Electronic and Bioengineering Laboratory of Stanford Research Institute, investigating the abilities of inexperienced and experienced volunteers to "view" remote technical targets, which included buildings, roads, laboratory apparatuses, and geography to determine the quality and accuracy of perception. In 1995, the CIA released declassified documents disclosing its sponsorship of the 1970s program of remote viewing, which was performed to determine whether the phenomena of RV would "have any utility for intelligence collection."

Programs such as the *Stargate Project* were kept classified until April 1995, when President Clinton issued an executive order entitled *Classified National Security Information*. It allowed for the protection of information to some extent to maintain security, but the documents' main focus was to create openness in an effort to emphasize their commitment to a more open government. Hal Puthoff, the founder and acting director (1972-85), was not able to mention anything of their programs until 1995 that would connect the Central Intelligence Agency, Stanford Research Institute, and Remote Viewing. Starting in 1995, he discussed the genesis of the program and reported on some of the early, declassified results that motivated initial interest. The program was a "multi-year, multi-site, multi-million-dollar effort." While involved at SRI in Menlo Park, CA, he circulated a proposal to gain funding for research related to quantum biology to determine whether the physical theory was capable of describing life processes, suggesting measurements involving plants and lower organisms. His widely circulated proposal met with the eyes of Cleve Backster in New York City, where he measured the electrical activity of plants with standard polygraph equipment. During a visit to Backster's lab, an artist by the name of Ingo Swann just happened to see Puthoff's proposal. Writing to Puthoff, Swann noted his interest in investigating the boundary between the physics of the animate and inanimate, and inquired about considering experiments of a parapsychological nature.

During their visit to the laboratory, Swann seemed to disturb the operating magnetometer, which was located in a vault below the floor of the building and was shielded by an aluminum container with copper shielding and a superconducting shield. Swann then went on to remote view the interior of the equipment and drew a reasonable facsimile of its construction. Puthoff documented his findings, which then showed up at SRI a few weeks later. Due to increasing concern within the intelligence community about a Soviet parapsychological-funded program, they were "on the lookout for a research laboratory outside academia that could handle a quiet, low-profile classified investigation," in which they would administer simple experiments with Swann. The tests revolved around Swann attempting to describe the contents of a box in which visitors had hidden objects.

In one test Swann said, "I see something small, brown, and irregular, sort of like a leaf or something that resembles it, except that it seems very much alive, like it's even moving!" The target chosen by one of the visitors turned out to be a small live moth looking much like a leaf.

The integrated results were impressive enough that an eight-month $49,909 Biofield Measurement Program was negotiated, linking laser colleague Russell Targ to the program, and thus was the beginning of remote viewing.

I must interject that although remote viewing came to light in the 1970s, it has been around for much longer than that. Native Americans have used remote viewing as well as other forms of mind control for thousands of years, but they did not use the label of *remote viewing* to describe how they could use their minds to travel through time, leave no footprints while walking, avoid being hit by bullets, or find medicinal vegetation that provided miraculous cures.

Additionally, researchers Robert Jahn and Brenda Dunne of PEARS at Princeton University studied psychokinesis effects on electronic random generators, linking subjects' intentions and random results. Jahn also studied remote viewing in 1982 and published a thorough review of psychic occurrences from an engineering perspective.

Inquiring minds continue to investigate whether a human's ability to perceive distinctive features of space was totally an acquired ability or was exclusively innate by way of some sensory apparatus. As described previously in the section on Cell Communication, we were able to determine that our perceptual, or better still, our sensory systems are fed information continuously because we are sentient, sensing beings hardwired as vast sensation-driven apparatuses, much like that of a supercomputer that sends and receives data twenty-four hours each day. Since we are bombarded with an overabundance of stimuli during the day, the question we must ask is not "What data can we obtain from our environment or things?" but rather, "How do we handle the stimulus or data the body receives?"

The answer lies not within our limited capabilities, but more so on the "what" we choose to focus our attention on. Any information can be processed effectively, impartially, and without prejudices, but in limited amounts. Therefore, it becomes essential for an individual to selectively focus on "relevant stimuli and reject distracting and extraneous ones."

Perception occurs through the learning processes, through exchange and familiarity with an environment, or "through commerce and experience," whereby one learns to selectively sense by shutting out all voices, noise, or static energy, except for one target of interest, by using innate but often not developed atypical sensory processes.

> "Such phenomena, although under scientific consideration for over a century, have historically been fraught with unreliability and controversy, and validation of the phenomena by accepted scientific methodology has been slow in coming...a recent survey conducted by the British publication **New Scientist** revealed that 67 percent of nearly 1500 responding readers (the majority of whom are working scientists and technologists) considered ESP to be an established fact or a likely possibility, and 88 percent held the investigation of ESP to be a legitimate scientific undertaking."

Delving into the distribution of sensation, perception, and attention one places upon the evaluation of a target, I feel safe to suggest that extrasensory perception and selective sensing should be included due to our multidimensional characteristics.

It is my belief that, as was suggested, proof has been established. Now is the time to focus on exposure and practical applications, which are the fundamental influences whereby we can sharpen our perception and innate responses. To assist in developing our innate abilities, there are individuals who offer training in remote viewing, a number of whom have modified or bastardized standard protocols used by the government or academia to serve them within their chosen fields of study, just as I have. In my case, I was moved to develop a protocol that not only made it easier to hone in on specific organs and systems to aid in the prevention of disease, but also to help guide physicians and scientists in the discovery of the origin of an ailment or imbalance. The typical mode of operation for physicians to date, due to the imposed restrictions of insurance carriers, has been in treating the symptoms of an ailment rather than in the treatment of the whole individual as well as the root cause of the illness. Over the past ten years, the focus has been slow to change, but with the help of individuals who sought to improve the patient experience, the Planetree model of care was borne. In 1978, the *Planetree m*odel of care spoke to the universal desire for comfort, nurturing, compassion, and information when patients were in their most vulnerable state. This innovative model was created for the needs and desires of the whole patient, which is gaining momentum and transforming the healthcare experience.

Chapter Twenty-Nine

Remote Viewing, Terminology and Basic Procedures

R emote viewing is a scientific approach to acquiring information that involves using proven methods to remotely sense or
perceive. It is an ability acquired by training. It is a learned capacity
to carry out pre-determined results without spending a lot of time
on it, rather than a psychic ability, although viewers may use any
or all their innate sensory abilities during remote viewing sessions.
It is sometimes an energy-intensive or initially tedious discipline; a
step-by-step procedure, which heightens your awareness of your subtle senses and intuition that can be used for spiritual growth, healing, and exploration. The viewer's experience can be mesmerizing (in
high resolution) and growth-producing, depending on what is being
viewed and how deeply they go. Practice makes perfect and, because

of the unparalleled accuracy, Wayne Carr of the Western Institute for Remote Viewing and Integral Healing suggests that this is one of humankind's greatest tools.

There are several major types or methods of remote viewing in which one can describe and locate people, events, objects, cultures, and information thousands of miles away or fifty years from now, because the human body, mind, soul, and spirit can transcend space and time. It is used for growth and healing, to explore emotional, religious, and spiritual worlds, and to obtain practical and accurate information about one's own life, medicine, the economy, the environment, missing loved ones or objects, and so forth. There seems to be no end to its applications and its potential for growth, healing, and exploration, which has been essentially unexplored.

Remote viewing allows the viewers to get in touch with a part of themselves that they may have never been in touch with. It is a discipline whereby one stays *with* their subtle senses in a pure and innocent way, without allowing the intellect or imagination to *jump in* too quickly. Combined with other powerful modalities, viewers can positively change and expand their consciousness and reality.

To get more familiar with remote viewing, we will investigate some of its terminology.

The *remote viewer* is the viewer or operator who executes a session. The *target* is the subject of the session, which can be a person, place, thing, event, or idea pulled from the past, present, or future.

There is a set random or pseudo-arbitrary number generated that is associated with the target and is used to provide remote viewers with a target number, which allows a viewer to remain unbiased. In many cases, to further support the integrity of the session, the viewer may choose to either be "front-loaded" or perform the session "blind" to what or who the target is.

Cues are sometimes given to the viewer during the session, offering fixed notions about what might be the solution or answer to the question or target's problem that needs to be addressed, while an *analytic overlay* surfaces during the session when the viewer starts to put pieces of the puzzle together and jumps to form a story in their mind as to what the target is or what the target is experiencing. It is the imagination that overlays the pattern of information that the viewer is identifying with.

Chapter Thirty

Perception

T oday, in appearances, we are in short supply of empathy, but we have never been more geared or better equipped to take this leap into amalgamating with and employing the body, mind, and spirit mindset. Although we are bombarded with tons of stimuli, most lack the know-how needed to fully grasp their oneness with the universal consciousness. Let us also add in the absence of parental guidance, due in part to most one- or even two-parent families lacking the time and patience needed to guide and help their children to develop into fully functioning, fully empathetic beings. I believe we should no longer discount the power of perception. Instead, our time may be better spent fully embracing it and nurturing our true gifts and abilities to address key issues in healthcare and guide others toward taking responsibility for their own health and well-being.

Wellness begins with education, and we should understand the role of intentionality, thought forms, beliefs, and the emotions we experience, based on the above-mentioned concepts. We must change our old, outmoded ideas around not having control over the outcome and, instead, recognize that we do have some say in how we are treated, how we act, what we choose, and how we encourage others to choose—in a way that will create health and wellbeing in all areas of life, not just in terms of healthcare.

Chapter Thirty-One

Stimulation and Sensations

A s we have discussed previously, the body is equipped to send information out into its environment and receive energy emanating from its environment. Whether the information is taken in or sent outward, it is the movement of energy that allows for information gathering, which is necessary to effectively stimulate each sentient organism.

The forms of information gathered contain biological utilities that are recognized by the body as mechanical (including pressure and vibratory force), thermal, chemical, and electromagnetic (including light energy). Each biological utility can act on specialized sense organs and receptors, thus transmitting or communicating information into the mind and body of another sentient being. The viewer absorbs the stimuli from the target, and it is automatically categorized or perceived as planes of consciousness.

In remote viewing, these planes of consciousness are labeled as descriptors, which can be primitive, intermediate, or advanced descriptors. These descriptors then evolve to leave impressions upon the sensory body, which were received from the target, such as **visuals** (colors, luminescence, contrasts, patterns), **tastes** (bitter, sour, spicy, sweet, stale), **smells** (fresh, pungent, fishy, putrid, blood, burnt), **dimensions**, such as *verticals* (high, low, deep), *horizontals* (flat, wide, thick), *diagonals*, (mass, density, space, and volume), **sounds, textures, temperatures, quantities** (few, many, one, multitudes), **shapes** (angles, balls, circles, amorphous, curves), **movements**, (falling, shaking, stopping, flowing, rocking), and **energetics** (vibrating, humming, magnetic, frozen, electric, vortex, gravitating, grounding, charging).

Should we willfully choose not to separate the body, mind, and spirit, then we would be able to use each to sense and perceive information as if the body were merely running a program on a supercomputer, circulating, distributing, and distinguishing data about any target it chooses. We would use every aspect of our being in concert to merge with or become the thing or things we choose to focus our attention on.

Chapter Thirty-Two

Space and Time

Variations of sense receptor structures and their mechanisms are formed by natural selection meeting the informational needs required for survival. All life forms interact with their surroundings, extracting information and performing some form of energy exchange with little or no concern with space and time. If we shift our perspective from disassociating time and space, and realign our consciousness to think in terms of everything being in the here and now, then there is nothing we cannot achieve, nor any information that is sacred or confidential. We need only hold the intention to connect to whatever information we need to gain access to.

A multi-celled organism's demands of interacting with the environment led to the evolution of receptor cells and units. Imagine how our receptor cells will change if we choose to embrace a new way of living to include the utilization of all sensory skills. Remote viewing is the tool to help us achieve this new way of living.

All living things have evolved over time, so, if I were to move across timelines, straight back to the Big Bang, or to look at the Dead Sea Scrolls, time and distance would mean little. I might even find a version of myself somewhere in any of those timelines and experience what environmental demands I was subjected to. Again, using RV techniques, we can view back as far as we like, see how life formed on the planet, who was involved in writing the scrolls, experience the advancements throughout the centuries, or we can move forward in time, five, ten, or more generations into the future, to see what life on Earth would look like.

Chapter Thirty-Three

Remote Viewing (RV) Conclusion

What makes someone a good remote viewer? During my interview with Wayne Carr, PhD, we discussed the need for well-balanced and grounded remote viewers. He suggests that a number of professional remote viewers had been pulled down the long, dark path to destruction, seeming to act strangely—almost paranoid—after being in the field for some time, quite possibly after a few viewers were roped into demonstrating their abilities to the media only to be unscrupulously dissected. They had been lied to and manipulated to discredit the field of remote viewing, while other viewers reported gloom and doom-type scenarios.

Two questions come to mind as I mull over the potential of getting caught up in extracting negative or incorrect information. How does one refrain from meandering down that dark road? With the amount of overall stimulus, we are subjected to the question of how one desensitizes to eliminate extraneous noise and static to receive accurate information. To be a good viewer, there is a need for balance. One must be able to determine whether what they are feeling is coming from within or from some outside source. We also need to be able to determine whether what we are picking up is "white noise." As you view, do not try to complete the story, or put all the puzzle pieces together. To eliminate noise, stick with describing what you sense. cellular memory communication and meditation are two other key elements in eliminating unimportant noise. Cellular memory communication assists its practitioner in releasing old, outmoded thoughts, emotions, and behaviors—obstacles that can keep the viewer from mastering the mind. Meditation, on the other hand, increases endorphins, which are a neurotransmitter that the body naturally uses to kill pain. They are compounds within the brain that act much like morphine as they attach to the same receptor cells. These compounds are responsible for happiness and are also a by-product of exercise. Research reports that the human nervous system is composed of a mechanism called the parasympathetic system, which regulates the heartbeat, breathing, and other involuntary motor functions, but also includes the sympathetic system, which arouses the body, preparing it for activity.

Meditation is another way to combat stress and static. Huff Post *Healthy Living* writer Robert Piper offers 10 reasons why every athlete in the world should meditate; however, I contend that meditation is not just for athletes, and should be used by those who wish to utilize the tool of remote viewing to surpass ordinary living or to promote health, healing, growth, and enlightenment.

The reasons for which Piper suggests we use meditation are as follows:

- It helps you focus

- It helps you cope with pain

- It helps you deal with fear

- It strengthens your immune system

- It hinders mind ruminations

- It makes you resilient

- It reduces stress

- It helps you stabilize emotions

- It helps you sleep

- It helps us to see our blind spots

I use this extraordinary tool to gather information for many reasons, but more so in aiding individuals in their health and healing practices. No matter what you choose to use it for, try to remember, "Do unto others as you would have done unto you." Remote view with integrity and always choose to do no harm.

When a client hires me to do a remote viewing job, I view or extract information rather than view to influence my targets. I have had clients ask that I change someone's mind or fix them in some way. That deprives others of free will. The experience I shared about the Malinois dog that attacked me is a good example of a human wanting to influence their pet's behavior. We both considered what the dog would be like if I were to mind-meld with him to fix his quirks. When I mind-melded with him, he was set in his ways, unpredictable, and would not stand to be controlled. So, rather than try to influence him using RV techniques, I mind-melded with him to hear his thoughts and feelings in hopes of understanding him a bit better for his owner's sake.

I was called by a doctor many moons ago to work on a blind target. The doctor provided the target number and hung up to give me time to determine what the target was and where it was located. Ten hours later, I scanned into the computer over 100 pages of information and sent them to him to turn in to the client. He called me an hour later to ask some questions.

"What is the target?" he said.

I replied that it was gold. He asked where it was located. I told him what part of the country I was viewing, what state it was in, and what the land looked like. He requested additional information on some of the pages then hung up to call the client back. Ten minutes later, he called to say that the client wanted me to go with him to locate this gold. I refused. There was no guarantee the client would listen to me, and I explained that during the RV session, a mountain lion, a bear, and a rattlesnake showed up. I did not want to subject myself to ten days out in the middle of nowhere to work with someone who might or might not listen or protect me. But after a lot of negotiating, I submitted to making the trip.

My husband went along to ensure my safety.

As it turned out, I saved my husband from a rattlesnake, a mountain lion and a bear that circled the camp each night while we slept, and the man did not listen to me until the last day. No matter what he paid me for making the trip, he had his own free will. I communicated with him each day, trying to guide him to where we were to search, yet he would call a psychic friend from his satellite phone and notify me that she did not think I was correct.

On the last day, just as I was packing our gear to trek four hours to the nearest airport, he decided to give me free rein to see what I could do. I put down our gear and walked the property to stand with my back against some nearby boulders. I closed my eyes and asked the boulders to show me where I might find something to confirm that the gold was, in fact, on that property. Asking for further proof initiated the energies within and around the land. As I opened my eyes, a yellow line formed that ran down the mountain away from me. I followed the line. The client asked me what I was doing, so I told him. He smirked and made some noises, which I ignored. I followed the line to its end, where I stopped and pointed at a large shrub.

"What am I supposed to do now?" the client asked.

"Dig up the shrub," I said. "We have to head to the airport so your men will have to dig it up without us."

"Is that where the gold is?" he asked with a smile.

"No, but you will find something that confirms that the gold is here on the property, and by the way, the land showed me where the men smelted the gold for transport. I walked to that area to point it out to his men, turned, loaded our equipment in his truck and said goodbye to everyone.

While waiting for our plane a text came in from the men doing the digging. They found an old pick and shovel under the shrub. Included were pictures showing more proof that gold had been smelted there on site.

I could have gotten upset about the client's behavior, but instead, I chose to put myself in his shoes. How would I feel if I were the one looking for the gold? Would I trust one person, or would I make the best use of any and all resources or people? Manipulating people is not the way I work, no matter how much someone is willing to pay.

New World Movement – Empower Everyone

Chapter Thirty-Four

Rapture, Leading Us Beyond Quantum Consciousness

Global Consciousness and Perception

It's natural to empathize with a fellow God-Human being; to understand another's plight or happiness in a way that can be both transforming and healing. For others to know that they have been heard and that someone identifies with them and knows them more deeply more often than not brings a sense of joy.

To empathize or feel empathy toward another is described as the capacity to recognize emotions that are experienced by another sentient or fictional being to feel physical affection, passion, and partiality. It is also defined as caring for others and having the desire to help them, experiencing emotions that match another's, discerning what another person is thinking and feeling, or becoming less distinct, becoming one with that person.

To consciously identify our own emotions may be an innate skill and the act of identifying them is most often achieved unconsciously without much thought, while more skilled practitioners trained in discovery processes, such as Cellular Memory Detoxification Techniques or even Emotional Freedom Techniques™, can willfully uncover emotions with striking degrees of effectiveness. To empathize involves understanding someone else's emotional state and is often characterized by bodily sensations that are often inexplicable. Grasping the emotions of another is central to empathy and sophisticated imaginative processes more essential to empathy involve a combination of one's own beliefs and desires and the beliefs and desires of others. Humans have the capacity to become familiar with the bodily sensations of another while also possessing the ability to imagine oneself as another, as we often do while watching films, where we identify with actors and their predicaments.

Researched forms of empathy are *affective empathy*, also known as *emotional empathy*, which is the capacity to respond with an appropriate emotion to another's mental state, while impairments can result in schizophrenia, depersonalization, and narcissism. Another form is *cognitive empathy*, which involves the capacity to understand someone else's perspective or mental state, and impairments in this form may result in bipolar disorder, borderline traits, and, in some instances, Autism.

The areas of the brain that are activated when one is feeling empathetically toward another are the *inferior frontal gyrus*, which is responsible for emotional empathy, and the *ventromedial prefrontal gyrus,* which mediates cognitive empathy. Interestingly, I have noticed while working with clients who tend to lie, that their thoughts and feelings about having lied activate a portion of the gyrus and often cause me to experience pain in that area of my brain as I take their energy in.

Author Jeremy Rifkin helps define empathy with his observation, "Empathy is distinct from sympathy, pity, and emotional contamination; sympathy or 'empathic concern' is the feeling of compassion or concern for another--wishing for them to be better off or happier." Pity, on the other hand, involves feeling that another is in trouble and in need of help when they are unable to fix their problems. When someone feels the emotions of another but does not recognize that this has happened, we label it as "emotional contamination," which is when they have absorbed the energy of another and begin to act as if it is their own.

What's the true nature of humanity? Some early seventeenth-century philosophers suggest that by human nature, we are aggressive and self-interested, born to fight, compete, and engage in relentless struggle to dominate and prevail. Others took a different approach. Locke claimed that humans are sociable and kindly disposed to one another, materialistic by nature, using our mental and physical labor to commandeer the quantifiable and reshape it into useful property to "optimize pleasure and mitigate pain."

In the latter nineteenth century, a new field of psychology was born, and scholars turned their attention to the musings of the human psyche. They wanted to know how the human mind worked. In this text, I concern myself not with the ponderings of human beings, but instead, I elaborate on what I know to be true, based on my own individual experiences as an empath, telepath, and practitioner of remote viewing, intuition, and cellular communication.

Over the last quarter of a century, I have been able to form intimate and genuine relationships, truly getting to know those individuals I work with. To use a term often heard over the years, I have been able to walk a thousand miles in their shoes. As an empath, I am able to feel what they feel, see what they see, and understand why they have chosen a particular course in life. To get that close to people meant that I had to risk being vulnerable. I had to be willing to lose myself to unite with their energy in an effort to fully grasp their "involvedness" in the world; so much so that I could not help but wonder whether empathy was innate, picked up through modeling, or a learned behavior.

It has been proposed that the newborns of many species of animals recognize a substantial amount of their environment with little or no experience.

***

Izaiah Justice Henderson, born May 25, 2005

I was in the hospital room when my grandson, Izaiah, was born, and I was the first person to make eye contact with him as he entered the world. Being as sensitive to energy as I am, I sensed that our energies merged, and I could see something in him; it appeared that something unspoken transpired between us. Perhaps he was familiar with my voice; we imprinted upon each other to some degree, or maybe we had known each other in a previous life. I am not sure, but I do know that there is a bond between us, and he seems to care very deeply for me and loves to learn how to do the things I have been able to do for people.

In his infancy, he spent a lot of time with my husband and me. We began using the "My Baby Can Read" digital videos with him, and by the age of three, he was speaking Spanish and English, as if both were his native language.

When he was five, I asked him to close his eyes, place his hands on his grandfather, and ask the body to show him any imbalances that reside within it, and then draw what he saw on a piece of paper. Interestingly, he touched his grandfather's chest, did his breathing exercises, and then smiled as his grandfather's body showed up in his mind's eye. He reached for the piece of paper and drew what he saw. The picture looked like a lung, but I did not guide him; I merely asked him to ask the picture what the name of the organ was. He replied by saying that the picture said it was his Pop-pop's lung. I then asked him to ask the lung what the dysfunction was. This time, he did not smile at the body's response, but instead turned to me with a grimace on his face and asked me if there was such a thing as DNA. I cast a glance toward my husband but did not miss a beat as I replied to his query. He turned his attention back to his grandfather's body and the lung replied that the circular-like object in the lung was in fact connected to his grandfather's DNA. I then asked him to ask the lung what it would take to rebalance. He replied that the lung said that his Pop-pop would need lots of nutritious food and exercise to fix this problem. Mind you, I had never done this with him before. He did not know what DNA was nor what a lung was, and I did not coerce him or give him the words to use. During this entire event, he spoke as if he were familiar with everything the body was speaking of and showing him, except for the DNA.

Two weeks after we had performed this experiment, my husband went for a CT scan of his lungs. The result: a nodule found in the left lower lung five years earlier had grown from two millimeters to five millimeters and to date, numerous other nodules have been discovered.

Infants younger than age one possess rudiments of empathy, but by the time they have reached the age of two, they display fundamental behaviors of empathy through emotional responses that match another person's expressive state. We often see this when our toddlers are seen consoling or showing concern for others. Researchers at the University of Chicago used a functional magnetic resonance imaging system on children between the ages of seven and twelve, who appeared to be prone to feeling other people's pain. The results were consistent with earlier "fMRI studies of pain empathy on adults." Additional aspects of the brain were activated when the youths saw someone being hurt by someone else, specifically regions within the brain that encompass proper reasoning. By age four, a child has the capacity to understand that others may have beliefs that are not like their own, also known as the "theory of the mind."

Although I won't delve into the subject now, I have recently been compelled to study Autism to understand what is seen, heard, smelled, tasted, and so forth, by children with this affliction. Jeremy Rifkin, author of *The Empathic Civilization,* suggests that autistic children have problems with understanding the principles of the test, which was demonstrated in the Sally-Anne test involving a number of participants who were introduced to dolls, Sally and Anne, and tested to determine whether participants would accept that one of the dolls, Sally, had her own beliefs that may not necessarily correlate with reality, the core requirement of theory of mind. Although this test was not conclusive, its application portrays "social development trends in autism."

Chapter Thirty-Five

What Makes Us What We Are

H ave you ever given thought to what matter and energy are? There's a distinct difference between the two. Matter has mass and energy is the ability to do work. Matter may have energy, but both are different from one another. To determine the difference, you can look around at the things within your environment that have mass and ask whether they take up space. If something does not have mass, it's considered energy. We, being made of energy and mass, act much like radio transmitters; we send and receive energy signals. I have spent countless hours testing my hypothesis about energy and mass being able to communicate with each other.

***

In my NASCAR racing days, I was called upon by race teams to diagnose their race cars during testing, qualifying, and before race time. In many instances, the teams merely needed to pick up a tenth of a second to make the race, so all I had to do was place my hands on the racecars or focus my attention on them to determine what part could be changed to get them into the race. Keep in mind that the tangible, touchable race car has mass and is made of energy. While the team members are building the cars and focusing their energy on them, it is that energy that brings the car to life. When I focus on a car, I can not only determine what's going on with the car, but also the team members that built it. The car will show me who is having relationship or work-related problems and what can be done to bring them back into balance.

Energy is the universal language and being such, it has ways of communicating. To those individuals who are more open to sensing, energy or the vibratory force associated with the target of focus can communicate beyond the range of the habitually used human senses. The Law of One states that there is no separation in the universe, everything is connected because the one true God is a conscious, living universe, and everything in it is a part of it and made up of the same material. In such a universe, humans and God are not separated; they are always directly and intimately connected to the whole God through the soul, which is said to exist in the non-material reality underlying the material world.

The God-source is in constant communication with us. Native Americans were familiar with this long before they were "discovered" by Europeans as they believed that we are all brothers and sisters, connected by energy and made of the same matter. As I stated, the source of all things is in communication at all times and it can take the form of visible light, infrared, ultraviolet, x-ray, microwaves, radio, and gamma rays, or other forms of energy, such as heat, sound, potential energy, and kinetic energy. In all cases, we can simply conclude that all energy and matter can communicate by transmitting something, be it sensations or images into the mind or body of an inquirer. Images convey a story, and because of this, they are considered a universal form of communication.

***

Parkinson's disease is an incurable progressive nervous disorder that is marked by distinct symptoms, examples of which can include trembling hands, shaking head, lifeless face, monotone voice, and a slow, shuffling gait. It is a debilitating disorder that also has the propensity to rob those afflicted of the ability to speak. Such was the case with my business partner's father. He was a tall and robust man in his earlier days, but when I saw him last, he had difficulty walking, feeding himself, and performing routine tasks that most of us take for granted.

Carol, my friend and business associate, and I were talking one afternoon on the phone when she relayed her frustration about the level of care George was getting. He now had limited ability to convey his needs verbally and on top of his Parkinson's, he also had diabetes, which she believed doctors were not adequately addressing. She was exhausted from trying to figure out what to do to help him, and while using my innate abilities, I sensed that she was expending too much energy on the negative issues. Her father had always been such a vibrant man and seeing him this way really upset her. As she conveyed the multitude of mishaps they were experiencing with the care team, she mentioned that she would really like to know exactly what he was feeling about the whole thing. She had been to the facility to meet with the team on numerous occasions to talk to them about the setbacks, but her repeated requests for change fell on deaf ears.

Feeling her sadness, I compassionately offered my services and suggested that we talk to George. She thanked me for wanting to help but reiterated that he really was not able to speak at length and felt that this might not be the best approach. Without pushing, I gently reminded her that I was telepathically able to communicate with him and he would not have to speak in the usual manner. She could ask questions, which I might revise to get to the heart of any issue, and then he could answer via mental telepathy so that I could translate his answers out loud to her. She seemed a bit skeptical and unsure but felt that she had no other immediate solutions. She would allow me to try. We agreed to meet at the assisted living facility over the weekend so that I could steer clear of Charlotte's crazy weekday traffic.

It was a beautiful Sunday morning and, as Carol predicted, there was little traffic on the road. We met in the parking lot first to talk for a minute. She had not told George that I was coming because she did not know what to say about my abilities. On our way up to his room, Carol expressed her uneasiness about how this would unfold. I asked her to relax and trust that it would all unfold easily and effortlessly. I told her to introduce me to her father and I would take care of the rest.

We entered the room to find George sitting up in his chair, covered with a blanket. His face lit up when he saw his beautiful daughter enter the room. He had a warm, inviting smile that fit the many fond memories Carol had previously shared with me. Carol greeted her father with a kiss and motioned for me to take a seat. She introduced me and I wasted no time initiating more conversation. Carol had told me that he had a lengthy career with the FBI, so I used this to engage him.

"George, Carol tells me you were with the FBI for a number of years." He smiled and nodded. "In your experiences with them, had you ever heard of the term *remote viewing*?" His face lit up and he nodded his head in affirmation. "Are you also familiar with the term *mental telepathy*?" He nodded his head again, still grinning from ear to ear. "I use mental telepathy to communicate with those who cannot speak, George. Carol tells me you have been having some issues with speaking due to your Parkinson's, so we thought we would find out if you would be interested in using me to convey your needs to your daughter."

George wiggled in his chair, legs kicking up and down like excited children might do when they cannot contain their enthusiasm.

"All right, George, all I need you to do is breathe as deeply as you can to get more oxygen to your brain, and I will do the rest. Carol will ask questions and if I feel the questions need to be reworded to help you clarify your needs more fully, I will do that. Are you good with this so far?" He nodded excitedly. I asked him if I could place my hands on his arm, which would help me feel and see more deeply. He nodded in agreement. I closed my eyes and welcomed his energy into a dance with my own. His love of dance came through clearly, and I conveyed what I saw to Carol. She smiled and laughed, offering that this was absolutely true. She was aware of her father's love of dance, and she had fond memories of her parents enjoying it immensely. I told Carol she could begin with the questions, and an hour or so later, we had harvested enough information to move into the problem-solving stage.

I felt his energy dipping, so we allowed George to drift off to sleep as Carol and I sat speaking about his feedback about the healthcare workers in charge of his daily care. Some had their own personal problems that they could not help but drag into work with them each day, which emanated into George's world, adding insult to injury. I took time to assess each caretaker remotely, using George's memories to connect to each person. I used great care to expound upon the issues each caretaker was having within their lives, offering some easy solutions. This helped Carol determine how deeply George felt for them and how he wished he could make their jobs easier. He wanted nothing more than to lighten their load and tell them how much he cared for them. Carol's anger turned to sympathy, and she was so moved by the information she stepped out of the room to speak to the caretaker in charge.

She returned to tell me that she had set up a luncheon meeting with his healthcare team on the first of the week and she intended to share her father's thoughts with them.

Days later, Carol called to tell me that her meeting was a tremendous success. The healthcare team was touched by George's comments, and they wanted her to come back that afternoon to share with the next shift. The faculty and staff were able to use Carol's information to transform the way George was cared for from that day until his last.

To empathize with another human being forces an unconscious understanding that their existence is as fragile as our own. It is made possible by the continuous flow of energy through their being. Although George was not able to communicate his wants and needs through verbal conversation, he was able to communicate via the continuous flow of energy through his sensory system—conveying his feelings and desires.

Allopathic healthcare practitioners today are only beginning to comprehend what it means to care for the multidimensional being that should be regarded in terms of the physical self, mental self, emotional self, and spiritual self, wrapped up in an intricate ball of matter, energy, flesh, and bone, whereas in the not-so-distant past, these things had not been their primary concern. Treating symptoms rather than the root cause was just the norm for those with allopathic training and an underdeveloped consciousness. To use a more holistic approach would mean that patients must take responsibility for their own health and well-being, but also understand that they are allowed to interact with their doctors to determine the root cause of their illnesses and to choose the best possible route to wellness.

Early in my life, I purposefully chose to develop my empathic and telepathic abilities so that I could feel what someone else feels. I thought that if I did my homework, I would be more apt to detect subtle and extreme imbalances to determine what each body part needed to heal. Don't get me wrong, in some instances, people need surgery, doctors, and medicine; but in more than 70% of the cases I have worked on, illness had been established on an emotional and mental level first, thereby causing a physical malady to manifest only after the patient ignored the first indicators that there was an imbalance. Those signs coming from the body are much like Morse code. When you have done something, said something, or thought something that the body found to be of no use or determined to be damaging to the cells, tissues, organs, and systems, it sends out a distress signal disguised as pain or inflammation to get your attention. This means that the body is communicating, and it may not be a time to run for the medicine cabinet! It's a time for introspection.

Whether we are dealing with the energy within our body or taking energy in from outside us, our sensory systems are on full alert, communicating continuously. When matter and energy within our environment try to communicate with us, they do so by transmitting images which, in turn, create sensations that are picked up by the sensory system of our body. To hear, smell, taste, see, or feel what is being communicated, one would only need to calm the internal chatter and "be" within a state of acceptance so that the images being projected register within the mind's eye for conscious review. Those who have not fully developed their intuition may not believe they can perform such tasks, but they might suggest that what they felt was more of a gut instinct or intuitive hit.

You do not always have to be consciously in a state of acceptance because the sensory system does most of the work without our conscious effort. When you are totally consumed by whatever it is that stresses you, energy and matter will still always try to communicate, and since time and space mean nothing to matter and energy, the message will register within the energy field to be retrieved when you are in your most aware state and ready to accept it. When, for instance, you are in a relaxed state and an image of a family member comes to mind, you think of picking up the phone to call them. Minutes later, your phone rings and it is that family member calling you.

***

While gardening, I often see images of people I know who are thinking of me. Since this has happened for years, I most often look at this as a system resembling that of voicemail. They think of me, and it registers in my mind's eye because I am relaxed and not thinking of anything but performing specific tasks associated with caring for the plants and trees in the garden. When I see their faces appear in my mind's eye, I send back a request: "If you want to speak to me, call." Let me just say, I am no longer surprised when within minutes of sending out the call request, my telephone rings and it is that person on the line reaching out to me.

We are truly a part of all that exists. Be mindful though; when we are out of balance in our lives, the energy within and around us acts much like a bumper car, thwarting all other energies that are trying to aid us in our efforts. When we are in balance, all energy dances with our energy, and so, the mystery has been revealed. What we focus on expands. Focus on the negative and we get more of the negative. When we focus on the good or positive, we experience more of the good. The same can be said for the human body. Eat more healthy food, think positively, be good to others, and more is sure to follow.

Chapter Thirty-Six

Interconnetedness

I n the *Synaptic Self, How Our Brains Become Who We Are,* the author imparts that all organs and tissues of the body are composed of cells, and that it is the brain cells that communicate directly with one another, whereas the other cells of the body do not. My view differs. It is my belief that the cells within our organs know their jobs and participate in a myriad of activities; they are interconnected to all other parts of the body and have an awareness of self, but they are able to understand intricate processes of the whole, while also possessing an understanding of infinity.

Energy emanating from our environment provides necessary stimulation to the sentient organism, which, in turn, act on specialized sense organs and receptors uniquely suited to their reception. Indiscriminate variations of the sense receptor structures and mechanisms are formed by natural selection to meet the informational needs required for our survival. All forms of life must interact with their surroundings, extracting information and performing some form of energy exchange.

Whether I'm working or not, I remain in a state of open awareness. I like to refer to that state as streaming. As long as I am open and streaming, my senses can detect messages coming from anywhere, about anything, and in all ways. A simple message that my mother is getting ready to call me presents a picture of her face in my mind's eye. Something more complex, such as a client having a stroke, presents the same responses within my body so that I can feel exactly what that person is experiencing.

I shared the story of our neighbor in North Carolina who had a gas leak and then had a heart attack. After her heart attack, her son called me to tell me she was mismanaging her medications. Since he lived four hours away, he needed someone to tend to her so that she wouldn't keep taking a week's worth of meds in one day. Since I was directly across the street from her, it was easy enough for me to take her medications to my house and walk over to give her what she needed. After about a week, she started getting irritable. I was kind, compassionate, and engaging as her tension grew. I wanted to keep the lines of communication open so that she would tell me when something was bothering her. This one morning, I knocked on the door, but she didn't come to let me in. The door was unlocked, so I let myself in and walked to the kitchen where she was preparing her breakfast. I watched in horror as she put a huge dollop of butter into a pan, broke two eggs into the melting mess, doused them with so much salt I almost gagged, and tossed two pieces of toast on top of it all.

"Catherine, are you okay?"

She never looked up at me. "Yup!"

"Are you trying to kill yourself all in one fell-swoop this morning? That's a hell of a mess you're getting ready to eat."

Still not looking at me, she snipped back. "Yup!"

"I'm going to ask you one more time, are you okay?"

"Nope!"

"Okay, that being the case, I am going to run home and do a few things. I will call your son to let him know and when you're done eating, I can run you to the doctor's. What do you think?"

"Nope! My physical therapist is coming."

"Alright. I will leave you to your visit with her and if you need anything, give me a call."

I left. Thirty minutes later, my phone rang. "Nicole, this is Cat's physical therapist. Something's not right. Can you hear her talking?"

I listened and immediately allowed my body to feel into the words I was hearing through the phone. "Call 911. She is having a stroke."

"How do you know?" she said.

"I can feel it. I am coming right over. I don't have time to explain. Just call EMS and I'll be right there."

I entered and tuned in to the surroundings, letting all my senses sift and stream through any stitch of information I could gather. I heard her gibberish coming from the living room, as well as the therapist on the telephone with the 911 operator. I walked to where Cat was sitting and knelt down in front of her. She couldn't see me, but she spoke aloud. "Oh, I smell Momma's vanilla cookies baking. They smell so good." There was nothing cooking. What she smelled was my vanilla body spray.

"Cat, honey, can you hear me?" She didn't reply. I laid my hands on her legs and closed my eyes so that I could see what was happening inside her body. My brain felt as if it would explode. I turned to the therapist, who was still trying to give details to the operator. "Are they coming? This is getting worse. If they don't get here quickly, she won't make it through this. She has a brain bleed."

"They're on the way, but how do you know she has a brain bleed?"

"My body feels what she is feeling. I'm an empath and my body acts like an fMRI machine. I can see what's happening inside her body and feel how it's functioning." Her jaw dropped.

The police and EMS showed up just then. I told them she was having a stroke and stressed the importance of loading her into the ambulance as they took their time following their normal protocol. They asked her to stand, asked her to stick out her tongue, lift her arms, and speak her name, none of which she could do. Thirty-five minutes later, they put her on the stretcher and loaded her for transport. The therapist left. I called her son and went to the house to get my car. Her son knew of my work and asked me to share my thoughts about what was happening. I told him that she wouldn't make it through this event and that he should get to the hospital as quickly as possible. I would go stay with her until he could get there.

When I got to the hospital, the ER nurse took me to her room and left us alone. She was awake but couldn't communicate verbally. I stood next to her bed, laid my hands on hers, and used telepathy to communicate with her. I told her that her son was on his way. I shared what was happening with her and let her know that the brain bleed was unbelievably bad. The bleed was so bad it felt as if all neural connections were burned, and there was no way for her to telepathically tell me anything. I had to rely upon my empathic senses to sift through her cells and pray she could understand the thoughts I was sending into her body. As tears began to fall from her eyes, I knew she understood. I told her that her body would not be able to fix this issue and that the doctors would ask whether they should do surgery. We had talked about her directives a little bit before all this happened so I was aware that comfort care would be the only thing she and her son would agree to. With my eyes still closed, I felt another presence in the room. I turned to find the doctor standing behind me, inquisitively assessing me.

"Who are you and what are you doing?" he asked.

"I am her eldercare advocate, and I was just talking to her."

"She can't talk."

"I know that, but that doesn't stop me from talking to her."

"Well, I'm glad you're here. I have been trying to call her son and he's not answering. We have got to get her into surgery now. She has a brain bleed."

"I spoke to her son. He understands the severity of the situation. They will not opt for surgery. He is asking that you make her as comfortable as possible, and he'll be here in about four hours." As the doctor ran out to get his cell phone, I said goodbye to Cat and wished her well on her journey home. I asked her body how long it would take for her to transition. Two days was the definitive answer.

Two days later, her son called me to let me know that she had slipped away peacefully.

Everything that we are, every cell within our body, every atom outside of ourselves is interconnected. When we are open and aware, data can be received and processed by way of multiple sensing disciplines. As we allow the sensory processes to sift through the data a story begins to unfold. In remote viewing the piecing together of a story instinctively by our brain is known as an intuitive overlay. These instinctive knowings pop into the mind with no effort and can be examined more deeply piece by piece.

When we are happy and at peace the interconnection occurs naturally with little effort, but what happens when you are employed in work that you hate? Or you're in a relationship that's destructive? Every bit of stimulus you encounter each day you interact within that job or in that relationship produces sensations within the body that, over time, lead to the physical body breaking down. Internalized toxic energy leads to stagnation and illness, and as time passes, the body looks for new ways to show you how unhappy you are about your station in life. How about your first experience with anxiety attacks? The body throws you a curveball because you did not heed its warning when it sent out a distress signal in the form of a headache, an eye twitch, or a stomachache. Look out; it's coming...it's coming, and then...*wham*! Now you're on your way to the doctor's because you are sick.

Can you say no to these sensory abilities? You can try, yet when you attempt to block them out, dreadful things happen that prove you're living your life out of flow or balance with the true nature of who and what you are. You can waste a lot of time being afraid and avoid using them altogether, but why would you want to?

People often ask me why I choose to further develop my abilities while others choose not to develop theirs. The short answer is parents don't teach their children these things. In nature the development of sense receptors depends upon the environment and what's necessary for survival. We are all born with a natural sense of empathy, but my choice to master my senses had been triggered by a movie I had seen as a child and by many undesirable experiences. The movie was my introduction to a supposed fictional character *who was empathic. I was intrigued by* the heroine and empath in the film as she touched people and took away their pain and illnesses. In the end, she had pulled a terrible affliction from a patient and could not rid herself of it. I remember thinking that I wanted to be like her, but even at that age, I was aware of not wanting to take away illnesses the way she had. Instead, I would teach people how to be responsible for their own health.

Chapter
Thirty-Seven

When Conventional Medicine Fails

Y our health is your responsibility, but what happens when you grant authority to a physician *that you think should know better than you?*

Many people think doctors know best. I too considered their 10+ years of education and hundreds of thousands of dollars it takes to get a degree. What most don't consider is that many licensed physicians may have graduated at the bottom of their class rather than at the top. They may have spent their entire college life stoned or half asleep. Then, let's also consider that they are taught a certain way, and most often are not taught much if anything about diet, nutrition, herbology, homeopathy, or other wholistic therapies and regimens. They are taught to look at your age, your home environment, your relationships and based upon those things, they look at three things that could fit into a norm. They are not taught to look at triggers—what caused the issue in the first place.

This is where I get on my soapbox. NO ONE should have dominion over you. NO ONE! Who gets to tell you how to live your life without revealing their agenda? And believe me, this entire pandemic fiasco is agenda driven.

The truth of the matter is, if you give your power away to them and you don't do your own research or inner investigation, you can't blame them.

I know, I know! Who has the time to educate themselves on the inner workings of the body when our daily life is consumed with what has to be done to pay the bills? If we were honest with ourselves, and we put our health and wellness first, ahead of the almighty buck, we would make the time.

Big pharmaceuticals are about BIG money. They do not necessarily care about our health. Drug side effects can change our life and body forever if we don't know any better. I can attest to that. I was prescribed a medication that almost killed me. My doctor wouldn't listen to me. She told me what she wanted to do, at a time when I had no energy to fight my way out of a wet paper bag. Then, after the physician administered the medication, I was left to fend for myself.

When I called the pharmaceutical company to ask them to help me get the medication out of my body, they asked me to hold for the risk management office. Guess who that was?

It was the company attorney. The guy had some big balls, let me tell you. He said, "Nicole, I am sorry you think the medication hurt you, but there is nothing we can do to help you and you don't have enough money to fight us."

Due diligence! Do not trust what anyone says without investigating all the variables first. Especially today!

In 2017, I had a dream. Not just any ole dream. I knew upon waking that this dream meant something big was about to happen.

In the dream, I was standing with a group of doctors and nurses of the UN. Children were standing in line and being ushered toward awaiting nurses with syringes. As each child walked up, the nurse would administer the vaccination. The eyes of each child would turn from a normal, natural color to silver. They were dying. My sensory body went to full alert when I watched each child die. A doctor walked by to tell me it was my turn for a shot. A nurse grabbed my arm and without making eye contact, said in a hushed tone, "You will not take that shot."

In March 2019, my phone rang. A man who said he was a doctor asked if I would participate in a study. He said I would be paid $900 for answering his questions and listening to what he had to say. Now, let me preface this by saying this was not a dream. I took his call and spent an hour on the phone with him and I knew there was something important I had to learn from this call. So, I listened to him. He said he was conducting research into how placing an object up into the nostrils would cause a person to sneeze and increase happy endorphins. That, in and of itself, set off my bullshit meter.

I listened to him. Everything he spoke about was controlling and manipulative, yet he tried to impart his wisdom about how no one should allow others to tell them how to live their lives. The longer I was on the phone with him, the angrier I got, yet I let him ramble on. When I thought I couldn't bear giving him another moment of my time, it happened. I heard a knock at his door, and he asked for a moment to let someone in. When he did, the man who entered said, "Is that another one?" The *doctor*, [if he really was one], said, "Yes." So, my bullshit meter wasn't wrong. There was something I was supposed to hear to prepare myself for what was to come.

In 2019, my cells told me that all lives would be changed over the next year. I was not to worry about where this might go but to focus on what I had learned that could be shared with humanity. I listened and quieted myself to get ready for whatever it was.

In 2020, well, you know the rest. Here we are. Trusting outside authorities that have no God-given authority over us. If you give your power away to those who haven't earned your trust, you cannot blame them. Do not be lazy when it comes to self-care. Your physicians may not be ready for you to interact and participate in your care, but too bad. Give them an opportunity to change. Do your homework and make them earn the money they charge for 4-6 minutes of care. That's the time many medical organizations allow each doctor to spend with each of the patients. Ask questions. Do your homework! Don't give in to a 4-minute diagnosis and let yourself walk out with a prescription that might just make you sicker. If you give them authority over your life and your body, you lose.

It's extremely important to know our body and understand how outside energy and experiences influence our physical, emotional, mental, and spiritual health and wellbeing. Focusing our attention on the prevention of illness and upkeep of the human frame seems like a more reasonable route to take, rather than waiting for the body to break down and require assistance from some outside source. We have a multitude of resources available to us that can be tapped into for self-care. Externally, we have access to others who have trained in specific disciplines and can help, while internally, we each possess special sending and receiving capabilities that allow us to extract information when we're in need of intervention. The sensory cells afford us these capabilities. You're in a power position, until you decide someone else knows more or better than you. You can either wake up and take your power back or request that medical universities and health institutions add intuition building into the curriculum for present and future physicians.

Chapter Thirty-Eight

Echolocation Utilization

N ow, after all the discussion about echolocation we've had so far, you have some idea of what it is. You may have even had time to practice using yours. Aside from the things I have done with my ability, what else can we use echolocation for? I have a friend who calls me regularly because she tends to lose her belongings. She called one afternoon to say that she had been outside working on the lawnmower and lost her keys. I asked her to focus, visualize her keys in her mind's eye, and then send out a signal of light to those keys as if she were a lighthouse searching for them. This, in turn, formed a line from her body to the keys, and I was able to see them on the ground just outside her garage. This technique has worked with humans, animals, and inanimate objects.

In another instance, a friend who runs *STAR, Save the Animal Rescue* in Waynesville, North Carolina, called because she had inadvertently caught a beloved farm cat in a skunk trap and released it without knowing what it was. She was hoping I could help provide some direction as to where the cat was heading upon being released miles from the rescue facility. I had her send me a photo of the cat and took time to connect energetically. Moments later, I could see the landscape unfold as if I were seeing through the cat's eyes. She went back to the location of his release and searched for this barn with the tractor tire against it. Not far from there, she found the exact barn with the big farm tractor tire, and the tire was leaning against a piece of metal shelving. She sent me a photo to confirm that she had found it. Inside the barn were cat prints. She left a trap, food, and a bed just in case. A day or two later, she called to say the owner of that barn wasn't happy, so she had to remove the stuff she had placed there to catch the cat. I told her that the cat was moving between that barn and another not far from there. She visited the farm next door and the owner happened to be a volunteer at her ranch. She allowed her to leave personal items on site and a day later, she sent a picture of him eating the food she had left. She confirmed that she had caught him and happily reunited him with his buddies at STAR.

In the aforementioned story where my friend lost her keys, she did not send out an auditory call by verbalizing what it was she was seeking, but instead sent out an energetic call via thought. When I ask someone to visualize a missing item, I imagine or visualize that I step into their mind, walk on top of the imaginary line I have asked them to draw, and I'm then led to the missing item and its environment. At times, instead of just finding it, I get bi-located and become one with it—inside it. My sensory system uses thought patterns for the purpose of orientation with little physical effort, although it does require conscious awareness and focus. As for a time delay, when I consciously connect with an object by using echolocation, it most often only takes a few seconds and up to five minutes for my sensory organs to receive the information.

Human echolocation can be performed by intentionally sending your energy out into the environment to communicate or connect with another human or thing—to retrieve physical, mental, emotional, and even spiritual information about that object. As I've shared previously, I use it to find and retrieve objects connected to another human to communicate parapsychologically, which allows me to hear another's thoughts.

Developing our specialized sensory structures increases the potential to extract information from any environment, no matter what that might be. As our range of functional demands increases, there is an even greater need to make finer sensory discriminations.

Again, Gerber's concept of vibrational medicine addresses the electromagnetic field, whereby a template is generated that regulates the development of health, the disposition of an organism, and its vibratory force. Our bodies, being the "multifaceted cohesive life-energy structure housing the soul and all its creative expressions," are able to decipher the signals returning from a target of interest through vibration, which can be heard, seen, felt, tasted, and smelled in the ultrasonic range, far outside the range of standard human physical sense organ perception. Shealy and Gerber share a similar view of the spiritual energy body, also known as the body's chakra system. These specialized energy centers throughout the body possess a "unique form of subtle life energy that is absorbed and distributed to our cells, organs, and body tissue." Environmental stimulation must reach the sense organs, and if we place our awareness on the sensation registering within one or more of our sensory organs, we need only determine where the sensation is coming from.

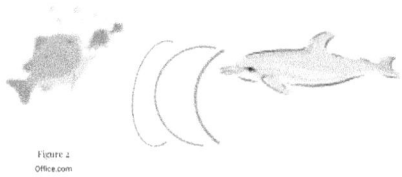

Figure 2
Office.com

Just as the dolphin sends out signals to find a food source, we humans have the ability to send out signals to "differentiate" what is within our external environment. The picture below depicts what the inquirer sees when sending out a signal that penetrates its target as they focus on wanting to *see* any organ or system imbalances within a human subject.

Figure 3
Office.com

By studying the bottlenose dolphin, researchers discovered that they are capable of distinguishing slight differences in the frequency of sounds. Their unique sounds change frequency characteristics as they send out signature whistle-like shrills, which are easily detectable by other listening dolphins: "Their inner ear has been modified to allow for the perception of high-frequency sounds that can reach ten times or more above the upper limits of adult human hearing." It is vital for dolphins to be able to sense high frequencies because it allows them to detect small objects such as fish hidden beneath the sandy ocean bottom. Recent studies posit that as their clicks strike an object, the echoes may preserve the spatial structure or shape of the reflecting object and may be interpreted by a higher center within the dolphin's brain, projecting images of the object they were able to detect. Echolocation capabilities are integrated with the dolphin's visual sensory system and are able to *penetrate* the surface of an object to reveal its inner structure.

Research reveals that dolphins may also possess a magnetic sense, which would allow them to use the Earth's magnetic field for orientation and navigation. Studies on this subject are still tentative and refer to correlations between regions where stranding has occurred in the presence of geomagnetic anomalies. Stranding occurs because of anomalies such as anti-submarine weaponry, which is intended to act against submarines and crews to sink vessels or reduce warring capabilities, posing a deadly threat to dolphins and other marine mammals. The sound, "thousands of times stronger than a jet engine fills their ears," which crews use to locate food, disorients, maims, and sometimes, kills the mammals. Evidence of killing radically surfaced in the year 2000 when four varied species of whales stranded themselves. Originally, the Navy denied involvement; however, after a thorough investigation, the government determined that mid-frequency sonar did, in fact, cause the mammals to strand themselves.

Chapter Thirty-Nine

Human Potential ~ Raising Humanity

We can now see that sonar can have a deadly impact, but what if we used it for the good of humanity and other living things? Fulton discusses the potential for human echolocation by means of which he compares human physiology and linguistics with the highly enhanced structure of the bottlenose dolphin—along with other members of the Cetacean family of whales and dolphins—in hopes of training humans to use echolocation more effectively.

Fulton suggested that children should be trained at the earliest possible age to familiarize themselves with the potential of echolocation so that the malleability of their brain can be engaged to magnify their inherent capabilities. Gibson proposed that animals guide their behavior by perceiving what environmental objects or encounters *afford for action*. The needs and capabilities of the animal and its environment are viewed as interlinking, and it is my contention that they should not be viewed as separate. He coined the term *affordances*, which is defined as "the possibilities for action that it offers or provides the organism."

Gibson emphasized the traditional study of the sense organs, preferring to focus on the information-gathering aspects rather than considering the sense organs as a passive receiver of imposed stimulation. He proposed a classification based on "modes of activity" and on the types of data harvested by the active organism, with the organisms' behavior being the central focus, looking, smelling, and tasting, which he believed would be accomplished by perceptual systems and the information obtained. An important piece of information within his works revolves around his notion of a haptic system that would include the skin, joints, and muscles, along with sense modalities, such as gustation (taste) and olfaction (smell).

Chapter Forty

Thought Transference

Telepathy, also known as *thought transference*, refers to the transmission of information from one person to another without any known sensory channels or physical interactions but can also be used to communicate with animals. To do so, one must be aware of what they are focusing on and be able to recognize and decode the data or sensations received. As multidimensional beings, we may use one, two, or more of our sensory channels during this type of exchange as we retrieve symbols, images, feelings, or sensations.

To refresh your memory, I include the four forms of telepathy that parapsychologists have described.

1. *Latent telepathy*, whereby one transfers information with an observable time lag between transmission and reception.

2. *Retrocognitive, precognitive,* and *intuitive telepathy,* which is the transmission of information about the past, present, or future state of an individual's mind to another.

3. *Emotive telepathy,* also known as remote influencing or emotional transfer, is the process of transferring kinesthetic sensations through an altered state; and

4. *Superconscious telepathy,* which involves extracting information from another individual.

What does it look like and feel like when someone is able to tap into all four forms of telepathy?

***

RV Analysis #1:

J. Austin, a friend of ours, called my husband one spring morning and asked him if he could help him and his father load a one thousand-plus pound calf into a trailer to transport to NC State Veterinary College. They had been cutting off the young gal's horns to ready her for a show when she got upset and turned herself upside down in the headstall. She was all right but not moving, and they feared she had hurt herself badly. Not wanting to take any chances, they decided that getting her into a trailer with the help of friends instead of putting her on her feet would be the best way to help her.

After Monty hung up, he explained what John had told him. My love for animals led me to invite myself along to see if I could help. It was a nice drive through the countryside to Marshville, and it gave me time to check in with the cells within my body to see if I could find out how this would play out. I was assured that she would load well, but the result might not be as positive. I tried to remain optimistic and inwardly focused on having a better outcome than what was revealed. An hour later, we pulled into the farm driveway to meet John, his father, and the farm hand.

As we got out of our vehicle, we noticed that the headstall had been disassembled and the calf lay in the field peacefully, seemingly unaffected. As we approached her, she shifted her weight, but she did not try to move her legs at all.

I stood by impatiently while the guys put together the equipment and tools to get her into the trailer. Not able to wait any longer, I asked for permission to walk into the field to greet her while they did what they had to do. John's father forewarned that cows tend to thrash when they're hurt like this, and he asked me to use great care in approaching her. I agreed and climbed the gate to get a closer look.

She watched me intently as I approached. When I was about a foot from her, I knelt, outstretched my hand, and began to breathe deeply to slow my heartbeat. She sensed the calmness within me and settled, allowing me to stroke her head and back. I spoke telepathically to her and explained what they were about to do to help her. As I carefully surveyed her energy, I asked her if she wanted to tell me what part of her body had been affected by the fall.

Her eyes opened wide when she heard my thoughts and she perked up, interested. I positioned myself right up against her back. I was far closer than the owner was comfortable with, but I assured him that she would not hurt me. I closed my eyes and breathed deeply again. Her voice was soft and peaceful, greeting my energy as I allowed my cells to communicate with her body. An x-ray-like vision guided me to a clear view of her spine. As I followed the energy of her spinal cord, I noticed there was a break in the nerve conduction to certain organs, and to her hind legs. The legs felt heavy and immovable. I withdrew from the vision as the farm hand was coming from the barn with the backhoe, and John was positioning the truck and trailer. Their idea was to move her onto a pallet and then use the backhoe to lift the pallet into the trailer to take her to Raleigh.

I hugged her and telepathically told her exactly what she could expect from all the commotion, urging her to be real still. I sent her the image from my mind to show her how we would have to flip her over onto her other side once we got the pallet positioned under her. She promised that she would trust me to do what was necessary. The guys were frantic about me being so close, but I assured them that she promised to stay still while we turned her over. They were amazed that she allowed me to jostle and adjust her body without thrashing around. Within ten minutes, we had her on the pallet, transferred both to the trailer, got everything tied down, and off they went to the Veterinary College.

A day or so later, I called to check on her, asking if a visit was allowed. He said that the Veterinary College was using hydrotherapy on her and that it was working. She was up, walking, and eating, and it looked promising. She had a fracture around the lumbar area of her spine, and it would be a toss-up as to whether she could be rehabilitated due to her size and weight, but everything was going better than they had expected. They would allow us to come by for a visit.

The care team had just finished putting her in her stall after a swim in the hydrotherapy tank when we arrived. She was eating as I climbed through the stall gate. She greeted me as if I were an old friend and nuzzled my hands affectionately. I kissed and hugged her while my husband stood outside taking pictures. I laid my hands on her and her lovely, peaceful voice filled my head. She thanked me for coming and said that she was not sure that their efforts would be rewarded. She did feel better, now that she could stand, and she especially enjoyed the water pool therapy. We gave her some extra love, said goodbye, and gave her the space to settle in and lie down for a rest.

One week later, I was awakened from a dream state with tear-drenched cheeks. Her tender, loving voice lingered in my head. The dream was so real. I felt as if I were right there in her stall with her, smelling the urine-drenched hay that was mounded and not removed from the stall as it should have been. She informed me that she had fallen during the night and re-injured herself. She knew her owner would choose to put her down and she wanted to say goodbye. She peacefully thanked me for being her friend and drifted off.

I got out of bed and called her owner to see how she was doing. He informed me of her late-night fall and said that he had no choice but to put her out of her misery. An animal that size would take more money and time to heal than he had to spare, which he was clearly not happy about.

I shared his sadness and communicated my dream to him, being certain to tell him that she was aware of how much he cared for her.

***

RV Analysis Two: Target # 0811-1952

Marybeth W. called to request an RV session for her friend. She asked if I needed any information about the target, to which I suggested that she only provide me with the target's birthdate yet left the decision up to her. Often, in remote viewing, to remain unbiased and allow the target to provide information that I was not privy to before the energetic connection, I opt to get as little input as is necessary. I allowed Marybeth to decide which way she wanted me to perform the RV session (either a blind session or a front-loaded session). She chose a blind study to help me stay totally unbiased.

I began the session with Dr. Carr's protocol, which I had studied years earlier, and then switched over to my own. I noticed that the target's spirit was trying with all its might to stay within her body. Body signals suggested that she was in a comatose state based on body temperature, pulse, respiration, and mechanical movements. She insisted that she had been in this state for some time, as if being held prisoner, so the underlying cause of her illness could be determined.

Nearing the end of the session, she telepathically communicated that she needed to know whether her body could make it through this ordeal. I assessed the body in its entirety, asking if there was any hope left that they could fix the issue. They answered, "No. There would be no fix, only release."

The final summary report reveals that she requested that her friends wean her off all medications, and the breathing apparatus, and pull the feeding tubes. Marybeth called a few days later to ask what was happening; she had not come out of the coma even though they did as she asked. I informed Marybeth that the target, Carol Ann, said that they did not pull the breathing apparatus and she asked again that they honor her decision. A day later, her friends convened at her bedside and did as Carol Ann requested. Within a few hours, she peacefully departed her body.

Chapter Forty-One

The Building Blocks of Life

"R espect and appreciate that you are the only You who will ever be here in this particular time and place; for in one second, you will be changed forever." Nicole Myers Henderson

As described previously Robert Hooke's discovery of the cell was a giant step forward in our evolution as he uncovered that it was the smallest, basic, biological structural and functional unit of life, of all known living organisms, further referred to as the "building blocks of life."

It's my belief that intuitive or remote viewing practitioners can know the body in its entirety, not necessarily as a result of being educated in the sciences per se, although it is helpful, but they can most often discern body parts by deeply listening and viewing information that comes from within the body in question. Communicating in such a way allows the viewer to sense exactly what areas of the body need attention and aids us in understanding what each system does so that we can better guide and assist healthcare practitioners and patients.

Aside from the known functions of each organ and system, each possesses the ability to sense energies at a much deeper level. The physical frame in part and in its entirety evolved to act in synergy with not only the body, mind, and spirit of each individual, but also all other life and things within its sphere of influence.

No matter what we choose to focus our energy on, we should recognize that all parts of the body maintain constant contact, communicating with each other, and knowing exactly how to act with or react to any given stimulus, whether it comes from inside or outside itself. Thinking of the body in this way generates images of universes within universes that communicate with and within one another.

Chapter Forty-Two

Cell Metabolism

There is a normal process of building up and breaking down of cells within the body known as metabolism, which can refer to all chemical reactions that occur within all living organisms including digestion and transportation of substances into and between different cells. These enzyme-catalyzed reactions, called intermediate metabolism, "allow organisms to grow and reproduce, maintain their structures, and respond to their environment." Two classifications of metabolism are 1) *catabolism*, which breaks down organic matter and harvests the energy via cellular respiration needed by anabolic reactions, and 2) *anabolism*, which uses the energy to build proteins and nucleic acids, which are components of cells.

Chemical reactions are organized into metabolic pathways, whereby one chemical is altered or transformed into another by a sequence of enzymes that are crucial to metabolism. The sequence of enzymes allows organisms to initiate necessary reactions that require energy that would not otherwise occur on their own. The reactions cause energy to be released.

This catalyst caused by these enzymes allows reactions to ensue more quickly and allows for the regulation of metabolic pathways in response to changes within the cell's environment or to signals from other cells. Cell signaling is part of a multifaceted system of communication governing cell activities and the coordination of cell actions.

"The cell has the ability to perceive and correctly respond to their microenvironment for the purposes of development, tissue repair, and immunity, as well as normal tissue homeostasis. Errors in cellular information processing are responsible for diseases such as cancer, autoimmunity, and diabetes. By understanding cell signaling, diseases may be treated effectively.

Chapter Forty-Three

Cell Storage

I propose that the cells of the body act as a storage system that captures our experiences every millisecond of every day. When we get overloaded or stressed, these cells send out warning signals to tell us that they are unhappy or overloaded, thus requiring our attention to relieve any conflict they may be experiencing. These signals may take the shape of unbridled emotions. They may appear as nervous-like twitches, shaking, or some other involuntary body movement. It may feel like a pain, sharp, stabbing, chronic, radiating. Fibromyalgia, Chronic fatigue syndrome, bronchitis, post-traumatic stress disorder, or it may simply feel like a minor discomfort. Based on individual experiences, as well as many years of working with clients using this mode of communication, I have found that most illnesses manifest on an emotional level first and then shift into the physical, presenting as an ailment, pain, or illness. The shift from emotional to physical tends to happen when we unknowingly dismiss the signals being transmitted by the body. If we were more mindful, awake, and aware of this, we would understand that we could head off a physical malady early on. The signals being transmitted signify a time of ripeness within the body. It is indicative of our body being able to change its molecular structure to bring about homeostasis. If you choose to communicate with the signals, the body stands a better chance of rebalancing the energy of your cells so that physical illness does not manifest, or so that the body can heal more quickly

Bridging the body and the mind, thus instigating cellular communication, is not that difficult. How will you know if you are applying the techniques correctly? There is really no right or wrong way to do this work. Everyone will have their own way of listening and their own way of applying what they hear from within. As you become more familiar with your body, you will know what is considered *normal* for you and what isn't. No two people will experience the same thing as they apply these techniques.

Chapter Forty-Four

God-Human and the Source

The evolution of life is ongoing, and all things evolve as the environment changes. That's just nature, and humans are poised for the next great leap in consciousness, into the God-Human era. This is the human who makes revolutionary advancements to *see* the next level, to go beyond what exists today, and to use all their faculties for the betterment of humanity. The God-Human is not a follower; instead, this God-Human looks for more information and puts mental puzzle pieces together, integrating and making breakthroughs while realizing that the only boundaries that exist in today's world are those that we perceive.

When the body is out of balance, the God-Human can turn inward and hear the *calls* echoing from within, listening to the signals and seeking to know and be better. When something is out of balance in the external environment, one need only quiet the mind and send out a *call* to question what it will take to put the environment back into balance. Sometimes, we will want to see what imbalances exist, and in other cases, as we get used to receiving guidance by tapping into our God-Human, we will leave the details alone and move forward toward the solution without wasting any time, thus causing a detoxifying effect and *cellular regeneration*.

That being mentioned, I do not believe God-human abilities are new. Each body has possessed these faculties from birth since the beginning of time, as individuals during the time of *Jesus* may have experienced. I would instead consider that the newness is related to the fact that we are only now more prepared to grasp the concept and use these abilities for the betterment of all life, no matter whether humanity is on the brink of self-induced extinction, or the Earth is ready to crumble under our feet. What matters now is our readiness to take this leap into the next phase of consciousness.

To be your God-self means that you willfully choose to fully integrate into the life experience and remain open to dance with all energies of this and other worlds. To be in touch with our God-Human persona, one need only consider that humans and all other life forms are created in the image of God. The "flame of God burns within each and every living thing. Each person, without the aid of a priest or religious institution has the ability to receive revelations from the God-source by discovering his own soul connection to the divine." Further, in the cited text, it is written that Jesus declared that the kingdom of God is within us as well as outside us, and when we come to know ourselves, we will realize that "we are the sons of the living father."

The Law of One is a concept that was ancient even during the time of Jesus and it possessed one single principle: "There is no separation in the universe. Everything is connected because the one true God is conscious living universe, and everything in it is a part of it and made up of the same material. In such a universe Human and God are not separated. They are always directly and intimately connected to the whole God through the soul which exists in the non-material reality underlying the material world."

I contend that there are two ways the cells of the body can be affected adversely: 1) Personal experience. Over time, our bodies become overwrought with emotions related to past events and act out to show us that they are not capable of working at optimum capacity, and 2) By picking up energy from someone or something else.

Our cellular body acts much like a radio transmitter or satellite that sends and receives energy signals. When one body is sending energy out, there is yet another that is open and ready to receive the signals coming in. Those who are aware will openly receive, assimilate, and assess the information and then simultaneously respond in answer to the energy that was projected. Most unaware individuals are not able to decipher the signals coming in and often misunderstand what they are feeling. When we unknowingly "pick up" energy from someone else that our body perceives as an undesirable stimulus, we would then internalize the information taken in, believing it is our *stuff*, which causes us to feel quite poorly because we don't know where it came from, how, or even why we picked it up in the first place.

Chapter Forty-Five

Body Detoxification

*C*ellular memory detoxification is a method or self-healing practice that I have developed over a twenty-year period, which has helped me in every area of my life. It is a way of communicating with our body systems and organs to assist in the freeing of **memories** connected to various emotions, past traumas, and experiences. The release of such experiences and emotions results in homeostasis on all levels.

How it works

It has been my experience that the body prefers that we take a *hands-off* or third-party approach. Most often, our God-Human persona asks us to view and listen to what it's trying to tell us. Most often, the body prefers that we not try to fix anything. It just wants us to see what caused the imbalance. By giving the body your undivided attention, it will bring itself back into balance with little to no effort on our part. If the body does require something from us, it will tell us exactly what it needs if we ask. But asking the right questions can be tricky.

Once you ask a question, it's necessary to assume the posture of a third-party viewer and listen. Imagine that you are visiting your best friend and you're having a conversation. You ask your best friend a question and your friend answers. You do not have to dig through your memory bank to seek answers. The body will move to answer you as quickly as you ask, and it can purge emotions and memories that are stored. As you chip away at the emotions and memories that surface, your body will feel lighter, and you will notice that the pains or symptoms have subsided.

Although physicians willingly educate themselves to help you heal your body, it's your life and your responsibility to tell them what's going on around you, what you're feeling, and what you feel may be contributing to a physical imbalance. It is important that you get more familiar with your body and find out what it needs and what it is trying to tell you so that you can guide your caregivers. It is not their sole responsibility to heal you. You should purposefully play a part in the experience and be willing to participate in your own rescue.

CDM Therapy can be used for many things

- Prevention of disease or dysfunction
- Cessation of smoking & drinking
- Eating healthier meals
- Aid in motivating and inspiring you to exercise.
- Healing from dysfunction and/or disease
- Recovering from illness such as Chronic fatigue syndrome, Fibromyalgia, chronic pain etc.
- Recovering from addiction
- Emotional and physical detoxification
- Recovering from war related illnesses such as PTSD, PCR Chronic adjustment
- syndrome, anxiety
- Alcohol, drug, and medication detoxification
- Compulsive buying, hoarding and obsessive-compulsive disorder, etc.
- Surgical procedures
- Pre-surgical preparation and post-surgical exercises
- Analysis of anesthesia
- Interviewing surgeons
- Choices in surgical styles-find what works best for you
- Post-surgical procedures
- Analysis of healthcare choices
- Choices in healing foods

Your cellular body can forewarn you of impending danger. Being connected to all other energy outside ourselves comes with benefits. If you are living in awareness, you will know what is coming and from where. Most of us tend to reside within a state of overload due to the stimulus from our environments. Electronic equipment, weather, jobs, family, and so on, bombard us daily.

What can you assess with these techniques?

- Relationships (marriage)
- Assessment of partners, potential partners, and dating
- Trust issues & jealousy
- Work related, associations, affiliations, & memberships
- Prospective strategic alliances & investors
- Future of a business
- Nature of business deals
- Family (children)
- Fertility & fertility treatments
- Probability of childbearing
- Defining family size
- Impending moves
- Resources you have at your disposal.
- Types & location of housing
- Religion (spirituality)
- What resonates with the body
- Places to worship
- How it affects your health
- Finances (strategic alliances)
- Seeking services
- Local offices (which to use)
- Types of investments
- Where to put your money
- How much cash to keep on hand
- How much to deposit
- Paying off debts (how much and how often to maximize your resources)
- Business & personal resources

By maintaining a deep state of awareness, you stand a better chance of positioning yourself to heal more quickly and respond rapidly in the face of natural disasters, allowing you to possess a greater capacity to assist others in their time of need.

***

While preparing myself for a trip to Tennessee to visit my father, I chose to sit for a moment while putting my clothes away to focus my attention inward. I questioned my organs to see whether they had any warnings or wisdom for me while holding the intention of having a safe trip, up and back.

My body spoke nothing in return but showed me a filmstrip-like view of me driving along in the car. I was on a steep hill, and I felt as if I was lying heavily footed on the braking system of the vehicle to avoid something. I sensed an obvious swerve and a sideways sliding action, of which I made a mental note. I decided that there was nothing I could do about it, so I chose to remain in a state of awareness. While driving up Fancy Gap in North Carolina at seventy miles per hour, everything looked quite normal, but I sensed that there was a need to slow down. I took my foot off the gas pedal and just as I did, a tractor-trailer driver hurriedly and carelessly veered into my lane without warning. I hit the brakes as fast as I could without losing control of the vehicle, and there was that sensation I had gotten an hour and a half earlier while questioning my body. Since I chose to tap into my source before setting out for Tennessee, and since I remained ever present to the dangers of the road, I avoided what could have been a terrible accident.

Imagine that you wake each morning and know how your day is going to unfold. That you may encounter Joe Schmo and Suzie Q Complainer and know exactly what you can say to help them with their life so that they become highly functioning God-Humans. Also, imagine that with this newfound knowledge, you can avoid potential pitfalls that could wreak havoc on your business, or better still, the economic structure of the nation in which you live. What else can it be used for?

- Investments: Try before you buy. Know what and who you're investing in.

- Investors: Will they complement your strengths and weaknesses? Do they fit your company profile? Do they have what it takes to see your project through to completion?

- Employee relations: Know the role of each employee; know their strengths and weaknesses.

- Daily preparation and clean up as well as the organization of your weekly or monthly events.

- Company debt and dissolution

Outside the business realm, we can also tap into things like skin disorders and wrinkle prevention to see what emotion resides within it and what memory is connected to that emotion that caused our skin to contract and fold. The lines on our faces and bodies are merely a roadmap of expressions resulting from our life experiences, not just environmental influences, and there is no limit to the knowledge we can gain by using these techniques.

Clearly, there are many ways to take advantage of your newfound wisdom. Begin your day with these techniques, use them during the day while at work or play, and end your day by cleaning up any unwanted energy you unknowingly carry around with you that you may have picked up from someone else. Success is realized when you understand your body's inner personality and its ability to handle any situation that presents itself.

When and how to use these techniques

Morning usage:

I love to start my day by checking in to see if my body needs some assistance or if it has some wisdom to share. Most often, I simply ask what I can do for God. Should you choose to start your day using these techniques, you can take ten minutes to gain knowledge, refresh yourself, and hear what your body wants you to know before you put your feet on the floor. This is a wonderful time to get a head start on your day.

Your body will tell you everything you need to know regarding your organs and systems. It can be specific about body parts, or it can use symbols to represent what the organ or system does. For example, a pipe may be the symbol for the esophagus or the intestines; a picture of the heart can represent exactly that—the physical heart or a matter housed in the heart. It is important that you pay attention to anything and everything your body tells you and shows you so that you can become familiar with the way your body naturally communicates with you.

You can ask questions such as those outlined below, or you can make up your own questions:

Is my body experiencing balance or imbalance today? If so, what organs need my attention?

What emotions reside within this organ?

What memories are connected to this emotion within this organ?

What roadblocks might we encounter today?

What kind of food should I eat today to best care for my body?

What color would you (the body) prefer to wear today?

Does my body want to exercise today? What kind? How much?

Who do we need to be in contact with today? (Or you can phrase the questions using words such as, *this week* or *this month*.)

Would you like to go on a vacation? If so, where would you like to go?

What is the best geographic location for this body, mind, and spirit? Where will this being resonate at its highest and best?

What is my divine purpose while I am here within this body?

Am I in the right job at this time?

Does this body want to heal? Do I want to heal?

Asking **specific** questions is imperative. Knowing whether the body wants to heal or whether you consciously want to heal will allow you to cut through to any deeper issues that may exist. Some people do not want to get well, even if their body does. They feel as if their illness serves a purpose, and they will be less apt to let go of it if they feel this way.

If your body does not want to heal, you may then ask more questions which would include the one most people need to ask:

Why do I choose to hold on to this illness?

What purpose does this illness currently serve?

Is what I am feeling coming from within me? Or is what I am feeling coming from someone or something outside me?

If so, does this person live close to me?

This is a good question to ask when we are around other people who are marinating in nasty energy. Since we are all energy beings, we absorb the energy of those around us. If you live with or are the caretaker for someone who has a debilitating illness, you may wish to check in regularly to ensure that your body is not picking up on that person's energy. By getting more familiar with the cells within your body, you will be more apt to distinguish what is coming from you and what is coming from someone else. By being aware of what is inside, we are less apt to take on the feelings of others.

If you wonder what someone else is thinking and feeling, you need to use care in trying to communicate with others on a cellular level. Be clear on your intent when you choose to ask questions pertaining to others. You should never ask questions about others when you are living in expectation of them. This means that if you *want* them to think and feel a certain way, you will most certainly end up feeling disappointed when you are faced with their truth rather than your own. When we live in expectation of others and ask our source for answers pertaining to them, there is a chance that our source won't answer. What happens next? Our conscious mind jumps in and answers for our God-Source, thereby offering information that is untrue because we are trying to control or manipulate the matter. My advice is to be clear on *why* you want to know things about others. If you only want to know something because you are lusting after an outcome, you should refrain from asking.

Key point number one: We must never use the information we are given to hurt, control, or manipulate others. Remember: Our energy moves out into our environment like a boomerang. If we send bad energy out, this negativity will return to hit you in the back of the head!

There is no limit to the knowledge you can gain once you have tapped into your own intuitive power. The more you use the techniques, the better you will get at asking questions that will yield appropriate answers. It is quite normal for you to generate your own questions once you get used to the process. As the body begins to answer you, you will learn to trust what you hear. Use your imagination and intuition, and let it guide you as you move through your body, opening its virtual doors.

Key point number two: Remember: If we seek to understand others and ourselves first, rather than judge, criticize and rationalize, all information will be revealed by our God-Source so that we can make informed decisions. In this way, we are *acting*

with life rather than reacting to things that are happening around us, otherwise known as *reacting to life*. An example of a type of job that fosters individuals who would be more reactive to life would be law enforcement. They act with life by performing their jobs as they are taught. They wait for things to happen so that they can respond or react to bring a situation back into balance. Once conditioned to a reactionary life, these officers find it difficult to act with life when they are not on duty. Using cellular memory therapy daily can help them restore and maintain balance, but it might take them a little time to adjust if they have been living in reaction for most of their lives. The important part of this crucial point is that there is no judgment, no criticism, and no rationalizing of what the body tells you or shows you. This is a standing rule when using CMD techniques. If your body shows you something, it is telling and showing you the truth of the matter. It may come in the form of images or be more symbolic-like, which means you may need to put the pieces of the puzzle together to understand what your body is trying to say. Either way, the God-source within us does not lie. It may be creative in showing us, but it is not in the habit of giving false information. Recall what Monty told Izaiah on our hike: "They don't lie." The conscious mind can be the tricky one, which is why it is best to listen to the heart and the body—the God-Source. Giving in to the conscious mind means you may end up meandering down the path to lustful destruction and manipulation of others.

Evening usage:

Should you use these techniques before going to bed each night, communicating with your source will help you clean up the experiences of the day, paving the way for peaceful sleep and a bright new outlook for the coming day. My body typically tells me what my experiences for the next day will be so that I can begin manifesting my desires while I am sleeping.

Key point number three: Your body can tell you anything you need to know if it trusts you and feels safe with you. If you make it feel vulnerable by disagreeing with it or being judgmental of what it has shown you, you will find it extremely difficult to get anything out of it. If it fears you or is angry with you due to past experiences, it may appear as a child or animal that has been beaten, hiding itself away inside your body. Alternatively, it may show up so that you can see it, but it might have its back turned to you, refusing to respond to your questioning because it feels judged or criticized by you. You may have also explained away something it had tried to tell you.

How to begin:

Begin by taking a full, deep breath in through your nose until the upper and lower lobes of your lungs are totally full. Hold for three seconds and then exhale out of your mouth until you have forced all the air out of your lungs (empty, empty, empty). Do this three more times. If you begin to feel dizzy, try using creative imagery and imagine that you are a tree anchoring your roots deep into the earth. Imagine the earth balancing and nurturing you once you have rooted yourself.

As you achieve balance, allow yourself to breathe normally. If you ever begin to feel as if you are losing the connection with your cells or your God-Source, I urge you to move back to your deep breathing.

Place your awareness on your body and how you're breathing. You are going to tap into your cells by asking specific questions. If you are asking your body about health and body issues, you can use creative visualization techniques such as this one. As you begin, imagine that there is a bright bar of light moving from the top of your head, through your body, highlighting organs that are interested in communicating with you today. As each organ appears to highlight itself, write it in your notebook. This will enable you to go back and review the information later, should this organ pop up again with similar emotional issues. Once you have taken note of each organ or system that was presented (be sure to write them down in your notebook), you will go back to the first one and begin the questioning process of each organ.

Key point number four: As each organ is presented, you may wish to begin questioning it immediately before moving the light bar to the next highlighted organ or system. There is no set rule in this instance, so do what feels right for you.

Key point number five: Trusting what is coming from your source, (the voice) is extremely important. It is the God-Source we were all given before birth into this life form. It knows all things, always. This is true for everyone. No one person was born into this world without this same God-Source energy. It connects us all and communicates with us all.

Let's just surmise that your source may choose to remain quiet when you enter for the first or second time you try this or even the tenth time. You've asked what emotion resides here within this organ and you hear no voice. I suggest you take some time to make friends with your source. It has been carrying that body of yours for however many years you have been alive, and it knows what it's doing. It is used to handle the foods, drinks, and medications you have been putting into it, fix the messes you get yourself involved in, and perform each and every task that each organ and system must perform every second of every day to keep you alive. It deserves your respect, and you may need to apologize to it before it opens up to you and trusts you.

What you can say to the source if it remains silent

Hello. I'd like to apologize for leaving you alone all these years to handle these important tasks. I am sorry for ignoring you, and in truth, I had no idea that I could communicate with you in this manner. I thought I was in control of all this. Had I known that we could communicate, I would have come to talk to you earlier. This may not be easy for me to pick up and learn, but I really would like to try. I would really like for us to be friends, to work together to prevent illness, heal the body, look and feel better, and help each organ do its job more efficiently and effectively. I do respect and love you for all you do for me. Will you forgive me and give me a chance to make it up to you?

Use creative visualization while applying this technique. Try to relax into it. This is just another form of meditation. If your eyes are closed, you may be able to see what your source actually looks like. It may appear as your child self or appear to be a certain age that will connect you to the emotion and memory that is stored within the organ in question. It can also show up as male, or female, or it may appear to be androgynous, merely taking on an appearance to act out the part relating to its emotion and memory that you are asking about.

Once you have made the connection to your God-Source, you should always be aware that it is within you. When you have questions about your life, or if you just remember to show it some courtesy (by asking it what it might want to eat during the day), this source of energy will become your best friend and inner guidance system throughout your life. It cannot be taken away from you, but it can retreat if you make it feel vulnerable, not trusted, unworthy, or ignored. It is extremely wise and can be very lazy if you allow your conscious mind to run the show all the time. Use these exercises frequently to maintain contact with your Source. You will benefit in a grand way if you choose to incorporate these techniques into your daily living.

Key point number six: Our conscious mind is the part of each of us who knows it must take out the garbage, take care of the family, go to work, clean the house, fix the car, and pay the bills. It is the very controlling aspect of each of us who says, "No one else is going to do this for me so I have to do it myself." If you constantly live in your conscious mind, trying to control every aspect of your life, striving for success, only to meet with constant barriers, you will have to be very mindful of forgetting your source energy. You will need to make it a point to work with this innate wisdom daily until it becomes more natural to you than going to the bathroom.

After you have made friends, you can go back to focusing on your breathing and communicating with the organ that you are going to speak with first. You can then return to whatever organ you are focused on at the time, and ask, "What emotion resides here?" Your source energy will answer. Again, if it doesn't answer, look for clues as to why it is withholding energy from you. Apologize and then focus on the list. If you are using a word list while asking the question, you will be drawn to a certain word or even a couple of words. Trust what you see. Your body just needs to find a comfortable way to communicate with you and the list may help it to do this.

Next, you will ask it to show you the very first memory, which is what I call the *trigger memory*, that it has stored within it and is connected to that emotion. It sounds a bit like this: "Brain, what emotion resides here?" Brain says fear. "Okay, if this is so, show me the very first memory you have of this particular fear."

Key point number seven: You do not have to dig through your memory banks to retrieve the memory. If you are truly connected to your cells, THE God-source, it will show and tell you everything you need to know. Remember: it feels the same as when you are having a conversation with your best friend. You ask the questions and your friend answers. Just as you could not know what memories are stored in your friend's body and you would not be able to dig for them, you don't know what memories are stored in your own body, and therefore, you must give your Source the same respect. Aim to merely allow it to show you the memory like a filmstrip, or just listen to it as it tells you what happened. It may tell you what age the memory took place, who was involved in the memory, and how it all

played out. You may even be able to hear conversations that your parents had while you were in your mother's womb.

Tapping into your source by using visualization techniques.

Some people find it difficult to take in information unless it comes through the eyes. You may be very visual and need this sort of stimulation to grasp what the body is trying to communicate to you. If you tend to absorb information via sight rather than by using your other sensory organs, you can close your eyes and use your inner sight to tap into the same information via creative imagery. I tend to use a symbol such as a house to represent my body. Focus on your breathing, as I have suggested previously. Once you achieve the body-breath balance, you can imagine or visualize that you are standing on your front doorstep. Reach for your doorknob, open it, and enter. Take note of what you see as you enter. Is the house in disarray? Is it a distinct color? Is it decorated differently? Does this inner house look different from the house in which you physically live? If so, is your body trying to tell you that it would prefer this house over the one you currently reside in? Pay attention to what you see.

Once you are inside, look for the person in charge of running the household. As you enter the house, you can simply holler or whisper your own name and request a response. Take note as to how that God-source reveals itself to you and take note of what it's doing as you enter the room. You can even ask your source what it's doing if it is not totally obvious. Have a conversation with it. Tell it how much you would enjoy the two of you working together and ask it if it wants your help. Once you two make friends, you can ask your source if it's willing to talk to you about organ and system functions, business affairs, or even personal issues.

You can use the rooms of your house to symbolize organs within your body. Water, for example, in the bathtub, may symbolize heavy emotions held within the bladder; a broken thermostat may be symbolic of your own inner thermometer being off kilter due to an infection or illness; the basement of a house may symbolize your reproductive or pelvic cavity; the attic may represent your brain, and so on. As your source guides you through your rooms pointing out specific trinkets, furniture, or fixtures, you can ask the source exactly what organ the object represents. You can look for bumps, bruises, and scratches. You can even taste and smell things or feel the texture of your organs. You will use a combination of your senses while working with your God-Human intellect. It may use whatever symbols are necessary to help you understand what it has been feeling and how an emotion affects that specific organ. You may find a few different emotions in an organ and you may also find the same emotion residing within more than one organ. Understand that there are many forms of each emotion and there will be many memories connected to those emotions.

The key is simply to pay attention to what you see, smell, taste, hear and feel. We were given these sensory gifts for a reason. Trust your source to guide you to the truth of a matter. Know that whatever route you choose to take to tap into your source energy really doesn't matter. Whatever vehicle you use to get there will work, just as long as you get there. The key is in your awareness and intention. What do you intend to accomplish by going within? Be clear about your objective. For me, it is about maintaining homeostasis—staying balanced so that illness does not manifest, and if by chance it does, it won't stay long because I am ever present in my awareness. Do I forget? Sometimes. Will I get sick? Probably, but I am better equipped with the tools I need to get well, and I am more able to determine why I allowed myself to get sick in the first place, and where I may have faltered in my communication with my body, organs, and cells.

Let's review the process of communication.

Once you get inside and know that you have connected with Source, ask it to identify the organ or system that needs attention. Then, ask it to show you what emotion is connected to that organ. Once you hear what it tells you, ask your source to show you the memory connected to that emotion. Now, you can either ask to see *the memory* or you can ask it to take you to the *very first memory* it has of ever feeling that emotion. There really is a difference between the two.

Key point number eight: Ask the source to show us the very first memory (the trigger memory) it has stored within that organ to determine just when that emotion was anchored. If we find the anchor memory and give it our full attention first, all other memories will fall like dominoes. The body will then be able to achieve balance easily, effortlessly, and typically, more quickly. If you choose to start with just any ole' memory, it may take you longer to regain inner balance. Be mindful that there are many forms of each emotion stored within our bodies. There are many experiences that your source will want to share with you. Speaking from personal experience, I have found it easier to go directly to the issue that started all the trouble in the first

place. By paying attention to that one first, all others will just show up for viewing and not wreak havoc on your emotional state. You should be able to view them with little attachment.

Emotions

If you have difficulty hearing what your source is trying to communicate to you, you may use this list to decide what emotion each organ or system is feeling. Pose the question: "What emotion resides here?" Take note of any words that stand out or appear highlighted. If you choose to use a list of words, stare at the list while communicating with your body; your God-Source will place your awareness upon the emotion that resides there. It may appear in bold print or a distinct color, or you may just intuitively know that it is the right one at that time.

List of Emotions

- Joy
- Knowledge
- Empowerment
- Freedom
- Love
- Appreciation
- Passion
- Irritation
- Overwhelm
- Disappointment
- Doubt
- Worry
- Blame
- Discouragement

- Enthusiasm
- Eagerness
- Happiness
- Positive expectation
- Belief
- Optimism
- Hopefulness
- Contentment
- Boredom
- Pessimism
- Frustration
- Depress
- Impatience
- Loneliness
- Anger
- Revenge
- Hatred
- Rage
- Jealousy
- Insecurity
- Guilt
- Unworthiness
- Fear
- Grief
- Depression
- Despair
- Powerlessness

Once you have determined the emotion and viewed the memory attached to whatever organ your source says requires attention, you can dig deeper. As you find your trigger memory, you can continue breaking down walls by asking the source within that organ to show you any other emotions and memories that are stored there that pertain to each emotion. There may be more than one emotion, or there may be more than one memory connected to that one emotion.

Key point number nine: If your body needs to release energy at any time throughout the process, I urge you to allow this to happen. Do not try to resist. By living in a state of allowance, the body can heal itself of any illness, any emotion, or any issue. This is the detoxifying portion of this therapy. Your body may need to cry, laugh, sing, cough, pass gas, excrete waste, or talk. You may hear sounds coming from within that you have never heard before. Again, I urge you to relax and allow it. If

anyone is around you at the time your body decides to let loose, just smile and shrug your shoulders! By judging, criticizing, or rationalizing what is coming out of you, you will segregate yourself from your God-source and have a tougher time when you go back in to finish the work. By allowing the release, your source will feel that it can trust you.

Key point number ten: If you have to function in a work environment that is not conducive to this sort of self-exploration, remember that you can tell your source that you need "this many" hours, that being however many hours you need to finish up your day, to get to a safe place to do your body work. Your source energy is childlike in the sense that it can get excited about having your attention. If there is an overload of information your source wants or needs to show you for your body to begin healing, it may try to cram a lot of information into a brief time. You need to pay attention to how you're feeling and how quickly you want to clean out your cellular body. Rest if your body calls for it. You do not have to allow it to get out of control to the point where you feel overwhelmed. Know that you can be the captain of this ship and let it sail only as fast as you want it to. Once you have dealt with one emotion within that organ, you can go back in and ask, "Are there any other emotions within this organ that need to be viewed at this time?" If your source brings up another emotion, you can then move to asking it to show you the very first memory it has stored. Watch, listen, and allow your body to purge.

You can also ask the source within the organ if it needs you to do anything about what it has just shown you. If it wants your help, it will tell you. Do not think that you have to do something. Always ask the source first if it needs your help. Be respectful and it will return the gesture. If it agrees to you offering help, then you can then ask it what exactly it wants you to do. It will be very candid with you and quite descriptive. Please remember not to judge or criticize what it tells you it wants. Just trust what you hear and do your best to follow through as is suggested. I spent two weeks crying like a baby and another two weeks laughing as if I had lost my mind while I was working on my own life. After a month of cellular detoxifying, I felt twenty pounds lighter and had no internal chatter going on in my head.

Key point number eleven: For those of you who suffer from delusions or hallucinations, I suggest you use the aid of a cellular memory practitioner until you have some time under your belt with these techniques. I have had clients who were diagnosed with schizophrenia who, during the first week or two, were not sure with whom they were communicating. They were so used to the voice inside being the bad part of themselves that they would freeze and need help moving forward. Do not fret about needing help. That's what caregivers are for.

There may be many emotions stored within an organ. Don't rush the process. Your body will do most of the work if you apply yourself to this process. Do your breathing, ask your questions, listen carefully, view what is shown to you, and document what you see, hear, taste, smell, and feel as you will more than likely experience it again at some point in your life. You may get so busy with life again that you forget to connect with your source. This is normal once your body has healed itself. We all have the tendency to fall back into old patterns of awareness. That's what comes with being human. The good thing is that if you do, you will be equipped to deal with it the next time.

These are techniques that you can use for the rest of your life, and if you document what you encounter in your CMD self-therapy from the beginning, you can go back and reread passages that pertain to specific organs and systems when something does arise. Those of you who remain mindful and aware stand a better chance of not reliving a certain experience again once you have made your peace with it. Awareness is the key component in life. Being aware is congruent to *acting with life*, thereby allowing a state of balance, harmony, and well-being. On the other hand, reacting to life creates distance, dysfunction, and quite possibly mental, emotional, and physical illness.

Key point number twelve: If you are wondering whether illness has manifested within you on a physical level, you can ask your body one further question: "Is this pain I am feeling emotional, mental, physical, or spiritual in nature?" If the pain or discomfort is truly emotional, it will tell you. If it has already manifested itself physically within an organ or system, your source can tell you what you need to do to assist it in its purging and healing processes. It will also tell you whether you need to visit a doctor and will be specific about what kind. Listen and trust the information you receive. There will be times, as you are getting acclimated to these techniques when you hear your body saying that an imbalance is physical in nature. Please know that most physical imbalances begin as an emotional imbalance based on our perception of our experiences. If you find the emotion and the trigger memory that sparked the physical issue, your body will find balance.

Keypoint number thirteen: Try not to panic if your body suggests that the imbalance is more physical in nature. All you need do is ask your body what it needs to bring balance back to that organ or system. What it tells you to do may sound silly. Don't despair; listen and be sure to ask more questions to get clear on whether your body wants you to help or not. To help may mean that you willingly eat a specific type of food or merely get some mild exercise.

Important: If you start hearing voices that tell you to hurt or kill someone or something, **call someone for help.** This is not something we encounter by using this process and we may need to dig deeper to see if some outside stimulus is causing this to happen. This has happened in cases where a physician had prescribed medication that the client reacted negatively to.

Our bodies are constantly trying to communicate with us. Our body may not like something we are thinking about, something we have put into it (e.g., food, drink, or medicine), something we said, something we are wearing, someone we hang with, or it may even be unhappy with our present job or life situation. If you are not truly *tapped in* at the level described, your body may be communicating more simply by using pain, discomfort, twitches, temperatures, noises, and so forth. You may wake up feeling great and begin to head out to a job you know you dislike, and *wham!* You immediately feel sick to your stomach. Most just think they have a belly ache and attribute it to something they ate; the normal mode of operation for most will be to take an over-the-counter medicine to make themselves feel better. Those of you who use CMD techniques will know better. As your body responds to your thoughts about not liking your job, and the stomach acts as the signal to get your attention, you will know to stop and take a moment to breathe, turning inward. It won't take long. Speak directly to the pain or discomfort. Breathe and connect. Ask, "What emotion resides here?" Then, ask the body part to take you to the very first memory it has of feeling that emotion. As you view it without judgment and criticism, the body pain in question will rebalance itself. If you choose to ask it for more information, be sure to pay attention to what it says, and if you make a promise to change something, be sure you are fully prepared to follow through. Trust is a two-way street. When you make promises to your source, be aware that one way or another, you will be required to follow through. Your source knows what is best for you, inside and out, and will hold you accountable. You will learn to trust it, and the more you do by responding to the information it shares, the more it will trust you.

Chapter Forty-Six

Heart Transplantation and Acceptance

Organ transplantation is an area of fervent interest to me. Specifically, I am interested in determining how cellular memory detoxification can help a new organ adjust to its surroundings and make friends with the immune system in an effort to reduce healing time and possibly even reduce any immunosuppressing medications used to lower the body's ability to reject a transplanted organ.

***

Eric Johnson was my first heart recipient cellular memory patient. His wife had mentioned that he was not feeling well, and after a few discussions about my protocol, we collectively decided to use my investigative techniques to determine what was going on and what it would take for him to heal properly. Eric wanted to make use of an approach that would get his organs to accept the new heart so that he could stop taking copious amounts of medications.

Eric and I met on May 5th, 2010. At the time of our first CMD session, Eric was feeling achy and experiencing pain in many areas of his body. He was rejoicing in having a new heart and felt that his etheric heart, the cellular energy of the old heart that had been physically removed, was in acceptance of this new heart, and he wanted to know what it would take for the other organs and his immune system to accept it, as well.

We began with enhancing his breathing and asked a question: "What will it take for the organs and immune system to accept the new heart?"

His body responded with the bold statement, "An act of God!" It took Eric by surprise.

Eric's lungs chimed in, "There is no problem here with the heart." However, they were concerned about the surgery experience due to feelings of exposure and terror.

Paying attention to my intuition, feeling and identifying the sensation in the lungs, I asked them to show Eric the very first memory held regarding terror and exposure. Eric then began to see a memory play out in his mind like a filmstrip, as if he were an outsider looking in on the movie of his life. He was five years old, climbing a tree. He could see the clothesline in the yard. He swung, fell on the ground, and knocked the wind out of himself. It was a scary and traumatic experience that happened only once. The scene faded and another quickly came to his mind. This one was related to smoking. His lungs said they felt abused.

I explained to Eric that this was a suitable time to apologize to his lungs and ask if there was anything he could do for them.

His lungs quickly replied, "Just love us."

As if the lungs were done, the vascular system, the energy of the blood, came forward. "I need the heart and lungs to work together in sync or I cannot go where I need to go," it said.

Eric suggested that the new heart had never been formally introduced to the other organs and they were taking offense to that, so I had Eric introduce the heart, lungs, and blood to see where the conversation would go.

The new heart also made the lungs uncomfortable, which resulted in many experiences with pleurisy or inflammation.

"What do the lungs need to reduce inflammation?" I asked.

Eric shared what came in answer to my question. "This heart beats too fast—in the upper eighty range. There is no Vagus nerve attached."

"Can I slow the heartbeat by myself?" Eric asked.

"Thoughts can speed it up. So, if I control my breathing, it will slow down," the blood relayed.

"Will the lungs accept the heart if you do deep breathing, making it more natural and more continuous?" I asked.

"Yes," Eric answered, sharing what the blood had told him.

"What does the heart want the lungs and blood to know?"

The heart said that it was trying as hard as it could, trying to fit in, trying to get along.

"Can you cut me some slack?" asked Eric's new heart.

His lungs replied, "Oh, I guess."

I asked the next question, "What does the heart need from the blood?"

Eric responded that it wanted to peacefully coexist. The blood said that it knows that the heart does not belong here, but it is beginning to get used to it.

"How long will it take for the blood to totally accept the heart so that drugs are not needed the way they are now?" I asked.

"Six months."

"What is needed for this to happen? Body communication or something other than this?" I inquired.

"It needs to not be afraid of the heart anymore," the blood responded.

"What can the heart say to help the blood with fear?" I asked.

The heart chimed in, "Can't you learn to accept my genetics?"

"I'm not programmed that way," said his blood.

"We are here to reprogram, aren't we?" asked his heart.

Eric decided to take the initiative and speak directly to the heart and the blood.

"Heart is your friend. White blood cells, I need you to love our new heart. I need you to turn off the signal that says attack. Turn off that switch and turn it on for other things. Turn off the attack signal. Each time you go into the heart, turn that signal off and stand down! The heart wants it done in three months. The T cells need to relay a message to the rest of the cells. We need a truce! The heart can be stronger and happier. The lungs can relax, too."

Comfortable with the progress made with the lungs and heart, we left those areas and moved to the stomach.

"What emotion resides here?" I asked.

We heard anger-noises emanating from Eric's body. When this happens, we don't try to stop it. It is important that the body feels safe and un-judged. It is best to let the body detoxify as it needs to, so no matter what noises come out of the body, we just let them come.

Eric relayed what the stomach offered. "I have to get along with that?" it says as it points toward the new heart. "I have to process all those nasty pills, too!"

"Are you ready to release and let go of having to do this job?" I asked.

"Yeah, I guess that is up to the blood, isn't it?"

Blood said laughingly, "You're asking an awful freakin' lot, Dad. Adjust to fewer medications, and I just recently adapted to prednisone being in the body."

"Blood declared a truce! What is our need for medications? Bladder and kidneys, what do you think?" Eric resolutely discharged inwardly.

"Empty me! Rid the body of toxins, and we will do our best."

We used this time to take a bathroom break. As silly as all of this might sound, Eric's body began to feel less tense to him with each answer the body communicated.

When we tapped back into the body, the blood still wanted to speak. "The colon is responsible too, you know!"

The colon joined the conversation. "I was half removed after the transplant. The whole ascending plus half of the transverse was taken out," it said.

"What can Eric do to help the intestines feel better?" I asked. Simply framing the questions paves the way for simple answers.

Eric replied, "They say I am doing a pretty good job."

"Are there any emotions there that need to be examined?"

"No, I've already dealt with that."

"Do they have any advice for the other organs?"

"It sure would be nice if you all got along. The stomach is dealing with the meds, and I have to thank the stomach for a job well done," said Eric.

As I tapped into Eric's energy, it felt smoother, softer, and more peaceful than it had when we first started our session, but there was more the body had to say, so we forged ahead.

"Legs, femur bones in particular."

I softly cajoled, "What emotion resides here?"

"We want to run away," said the legs.

"Show Eric the trigger memory that resides in wanting to run away," I suggested.

"I am noticeably young. I have this sense of fear. A very heavy fear," said Eric.

"How does this heavy fear relate to your life right now?" I asked.

"I feel financially trapped in this current position. I have no savings due to the need for organic foods and hospital bills."

"What is needed for the body to bring itself back into balance and allow your outer environment, especially your financial condition, to find symmetry?"

"Hold the vision of running for ten minutes each day. This will help rehabilitate and rejuvenate."

"Can you do this?" I asked.

"Yes, yes I can!"

"Your visualizations must include a fair amount of exertion; really *see* yourself. See your body exercising, legs moving, heart beating faster but normally, and see yourself doing this fairly easily.

"Eric, what do the lungs believe is needed for easy and effortless exercising of the heart to build itself up?" I asked.

"The heart says I need to strengthen the legs and get the body where it can move faster and easier," Eric responded.

I could feel Eric's energy waning. This was my final question: "How long will this process take?"

"A few months," his body offered in conclusion.

Although time should not be our focus when allowing the body to heal naturally, we, our conscious mind, sometimes want to know how long it will take to accomplish a task so that we can gauge our progress or regression of a disorder or dysfunction. Either way, it doesn't matter. You just do what you feel is right for you.

It has been years since I first saw Eric, although I called him before publishing my manuscript to request permission to share his story and to check in. He and his wife are doing well. At the time I spoke to him, he had gotten a new job with better pay and was still using the CMD method to communicate with his body. He's incredibly happy about the results and intends to stick with this technique to ensure his health.

The following pages are included so that you may understand what your source energy is trying to communicate to you. Be mindful of connecting to your God-Source first before you look at these charts. As you ask your questions, the source will lead you to the correct word that relates to the proper organ or system.

If you choose to focus on the systems of your body, you can use the following questions to guide you through the process.

Questions you can ask or alter:

What system needs attention at this time?

Other questions to ask:

The origin of the present condition involves which system?

Body Systems

Integumentary:	Other words the body may use:	
Skin	Cells	Mammary
Skeletal	Tissues	Thyroid
Muscular	Para-sympathetic	Parathyroid
Nervous	Chakra	Parotid
Endocrine	Sensory	Thymus
Cardiovascular	Genital	Spleen
Lymphatic /	Sympathetic	Lymph
Immune	Psychological	Pancreas
Respiratory	Circulatory	Adrenal
Digestive	Spinal	Ovaries
Urinary	Glandular	Prostate
Reproductive	(Endocrine)	Testes
	System	Liver
	Pineal	Pancreas
	Pituitary	

One or more of these may also reside within the digestive system, but I placed them here for simplicity's sake.

If there is a condition that you are experiencing

You can ask or alter the following questions:

This dysfunction is manifesting as what sort of condition?

- High

- Normal

- Low

- Acute

- Aching

- Chronic

- Sudden

- Constant

- Under-active

- Over-active

- Intermittent

- Insufficient

- Sufficient

- Deficient

- Excessive

Is it necessary that I assist in the healing?
Yes
No

(Wait for your source to answer. When it does, you can move to ask the next question.)

What can I do to help you?

Nothing or something else—please elaborate: _____.

What is the source of the present condition?

The question you can ask and scan over the potential answers to see which one stands out for you:

What is the source of my present condition?

Potential Sources of Health Conditions

- Diet
- Beliefs
- Past
- Karma
- Emotions
- Nutrition
- Toxins (internal)
- Heavy metals
- Land
- Air
- Water
- Electromagnetic frequencies

Other:
- Chakra imbalance
- Suppression/block ages
- Constitution/will (extreme or lack of)
- Color/light deficiency
- Allergic Reaction

- Influence by others
- Imprint (other)
- Imprint (mother)
- Imprint (father)
- Family lineage
- Spiritual interference/influence
- Unresolved spiritual issues
- Unresolved emotional issues
- Unresolved mental issues
- Unresolved physical issues
- Unconscious thoughts
- Traumatic experience(s)
- Surgery/medical procedure
- Childhood medicine/inoculations
- Bacteria/virus invasion
- Genetic inheritance
- Adult medicine
- Fungus
- Parasites
- Prior injuries

What, if anything, can I do to help you? (Wait for your source to answer.)

Nothing or_____.

What type of diet or lifestyle change is needed at this time?

- Mediterranean

- Atkins-high-protein, high-fat, low-carbohydrate diet

- Vegan-no animal products

- Vegetarian-eat vegetables, fruits, grains, seeds, usually eggs, but no meat or fish

- Other

The origin of dysfunction

Body Parts

- Mind
- Head
- Sinus/ Nose
- Mouth/Tongue
- Teeth
- Ears
- Throat
- Eyes
- Abdomen
- Stomach
- Rectum

- Liver
- Spleen
- Pancreas
- Kidney
- Bladder
- Larynx
- Trachea
- Back/Spine
- Heart

- Upper limb
- Lower limb
- Reproductive organ(s)
- Lungs/Bronchial
- Skin
- Nerves
- Shoulders
- Neck
- Tissue
- Gland(s)

Questions to ask:

The dysfunction is located in which part(s) of my body?

What other body parts require my attention at this time?

How to use your newfound abilities

What can we do with a more pronounced connection to intuition? My answer is quite simple: **anything you want**. I would, however, like to advocate that you willfully choose not to hurt others, trespass on their thoughts, or use privileged information to ruin their lives. Always practice these techniques while considering that we must choose to do no harm.

How cells react to stimulation

If you are paying attention to the cells and communicating with them, they are receiving stimulation, but cells are constantly receiving stimulation at all hours of the day and night. As described within part one of *Empathy, Telepathy and Echolocation*, we learned that we are capable of emitting sounds or sending out signals, which, in turn, will pick up signals and retrieve data from other objects that have been returned to the sender via echoes from the target environment when focused upon.

When we are purposeful in using the innate skill of echolocation to gain insight, it can be performed intentionally by emitting or sending our thoughts (energy) out into the environment to communicate or connect with another human or thing, to retrieve physical, mental, emotional, and even spiritual information about that object, to find and retrieve objects that belong to someone else, or to communicate telepathically, allowing one to hear another's thoughts and to empathically feel and understand how another person experiences their life. Even still, most of these things transpire without our conscious will.

Whether we hold with the concept offered by retired neurosurgeon, Norm Shealy, when he said that there are "seven major sheaths" connected to the living that have the ability to detect other energies in and around us, or whether we choose to follow the idea of echolocation, if our sensory cells are activated by our thoughts, then we are better able to detect more subtle transmissions of energy, such as electromagnetic radiation, radio waves, or even decipher codes, signals, or information from within another human body, as well as from the environment.

***

Gregg Spieth is a veteran who survived the Vietnamese War, which triggered a cavalcade of bodily reactions that resulted in thirty-six years of severe back pain. He expressed an interest in sharing his wartime experience to help others see that they do not have to live with debilitating pain.

Gregg entered with extreme back pain, stating that he had seen every type of doctor that he could think of, and up to that point, had gotten no relief from any of the modalities or medication prescribed to treat him.

By intentionally activating the sensory cells within my body, I focused on asking the cells within his body to show me the origin of his dysfunction. The information that echoed back into my cells revealed that his back pain was only a secondary imbalance and that the *trigger* resided within his stomach. I then sent out another call or question, asking the stomach to tell me what emotion resided within it that was causing this dysfunction. The information my cells retrieved suggested that the imbalance within his stomach was a result of guilt and food.

I turned my attention to Gregg to engage him in the process of communicating with the sensory cells within his body. I told Gregg what his body said about the back pain not being the primary imbalance and that it was his stomach instead, along with a memory regarding food. He grew angry, so I asked him to keep an open mind and try to allow the body to communicate with us without fear of judgment, criticism, or rationalizations. Although he did not understand the process, he agreed to try. After some deep breathing exercises, Gregg closed his eyes, and I began asking specific questions.

"What emotions reside within the stomach? "

"Fear and guilt," he answered.

Next, I asked his body to take him to the very first memory the stomach ever had in regard to fear around food. In answer to my inquiry, Gregg acted as if a bomb went off inside his body as he was mentally transported back to Vietnam, where he and his platoon were starving. He and one other officer agreed to venture out into the bomb trenches to forage for food for everyone. At this juncture, Gregg became visibly emotional, and he began to sob relentlessly. He relayed the filmstrip-like memory as he gasped for air, saying that as he and his comrades moved through the trenches, eating some of the food they found before taking any back to the platoon. He had internalized his guilt, and this is when the back pain began. In response to our questioning and holding a space to view the experiences without trying to fix the problem, his back pain disappeared instantly, and it has not returned since.

I reiterate that my belief is that physical bodily sensations are codes or distress signals that the cells within our body send out in response to a particular stimulus, such as our thoughts or actions, the result of our mental beliefs, and the emotions that we experience at the peak of a specific event. If we focus on the one cause rather than the presenting ailment of any one illness, and if one intentionally looks for that one cause, we will find that it is the accretion of all factors, physical, mental, emotional, spiritual, chemical, and electromagnetic, that will determine the health of the physical form.

As we decipher the signals returning from our target of focus, our sensory cells share information that can be heard, seen, felt, tasted, and smelled, in the ultrasonic range, far outside the range of ordinary human physical sense organs.

As multidimensional beings, our physical, mental, emotional, and spiritual characteristics are divinely interwoven, creating a matrix, which has the capacity to either create or disrupt currents of energy. In either case, our energy extends outward, instigating an effect that impacts our target of focus, or our external environment, either positively or negatively, while our inner environment is being bombarded by the stimulus from the external world.

An example of a disruption in energy current is organ failure. When an organ has experienced trauma and surgeons decide that a transplant is beneficial for the patient, there's more to consider. There is the energy of the life and their experiences that are stored in that organ. If you move an organ from one body to another, the life experiences move with it and cannot be deleted or dismissed. What's stored within the cells of the organ that is going to be transplanted from the giver to its new host, is called cellular memory. Everything the giver was, will become a part of the recipient, like it or not: "Cellular memory is the hypothesis that such things as memories, habits, interests, and tastes may somehow be stored in all the cells of human bodies, not only in the brain...evidence of which revolves around organ transplants after which the recipient was reported to have developed new habits or memories."

Posted from the same text are the reports of how cellular memory can be affected directly if the physical body is altered in any way.

An article published in 2000 in *Integrative Medicine,* a short-lived alternative therapy journal, reported stories of organ recipients who inherited such traits as a love for classical music, a change of sexual orientation, and changes in diet and vocabulary. To date, there has been no case where personality traits or memories have been passed from donor to recipient following an organ transplant, nor has one ever been recorded in a peer-reviewed medical or scientific journal, yet I believe there is reason for further study of this subject.

I do not consider myself a panic peddler, yet I cannot help considering some things related to this topic. Like, what if a transplant recipient was asked if they noticed any new behaviors or traits after surgery? What if their new life confirms that the inherent traits of the donor are integrated into the recipient? Further, what if an organ recipient receives an organ from someone who lived an extremely hard life? If due to their negative life experiences, they were considered psychologically damaged or they possessed the personality traits of a person that would, could, or had hurt others.

To help you understand how energy is transferred let's try imagining a situation a lot less serious than an organ transplant.

When I went to Washington State to enhance my knowledge of remote viewing, I decided to treat myself to a massage. Being empathic means that, when someone touches me, their energy flows over into my body to be assessed. Knowing that my body does that naturally, I chose to request information about all of their therapists so that I could choose one who wasn't a walking *Jerry Springer Show*. If they were high drama, what was supposed to be a relaxing experience for me would turn into a torture session and I would walk away feeling like someone dumped all their garbage on me. My decision to assess therapists proved correct.

Communicating with body cells may seem unnatural to some, but it's easy for me to trust and believe the answers that come from this form of exchange because time and time again, the information received has been valid. With time comes comfort and trust. When I receive answers, I have no reason to doubt what I hear. Those new to this concept will learn how to trust their cellular body with practice.

The process is quite simple. You think of a question that you need answered and the cells within your organs and systems respond. The answers may take the form of intuitive knowing or gut feelings, pain, discomfort, and may even present as a disease. When the cells become overwrought, we can communicate via the process of cellular memory detoxification, which I created many years ago to help the body restore balance.

Chapter Forty-Seven

Cell Communication Synopsis

Everything around us and within us communicates with everything else. When we get overloaded or stressed, the cells send out signals to tell us that they are unhappy or overloaded, thus requiring our attention to relieve any conflict they may be experiencing. If these bodily reactions were triggered by our perception or our sensory cells' perception of an event that transpires, any of these imbalances may be strictly emotional in nature rather than a potentially inflexible physical ailment. Within my professional practice, I have worked with individuals who had developed maladies on the physical plane and the cells were still able to restore balance, thus liberating the organ or system.

I feel it worthwhile to mention this again. Cells are able to communicate with one another to perform intricate functions and it stands to reason that we, being of divine consciousness, have the ability to focus our awareness upon any one thing and extract information that will assist the body in reestablishing homeostasis on its own without external intervention, unless it becomes necessary.

Energy signatures transferred from one person to another are therefore unconsciously assimilated by performing such an act. After having used this form of communication for most of my adult life, I personally believe that we, as multidimensional beings, may use one, two, or more of our sensory channels during this type of exchange as information is retrieved in sensations, symbols and images, or type-written words.

From our head to our feet, to the afferent and efferent pathways of the spinal cord, to the epidermis of the integumentary system, or to the innermost workings of the cell, **we are sensory,** and to establish the new God-Human civilization whereby each uses their innate abilities, we must cut through the noise, static, and life stresses to center or focus oneself on a particular target without letting the ego participate.

Remote viewing applications allow for this nature of centering to occur. The techniques and protocols allow conscious, sentient beings to tap into any environment at will and extract information, allowing the viewer to intimately and genuinely know someone, to walk a thousand miles in their shoes, to feel what they feel, to see what they see, to understand what is going on in their present life, and to even determine why they have chosen a particular course in life. The viewer can get so close to someone that they can become one with the target, fully grasping the target's involvement in the world. Remote viewing is an instrument, a tool that allows us to take a leap into oneness with all that exists for the purposes of acquiring or expanding one's consciousness, thus merging with the quantum consciousness for communication, healing, growth, and enlightenment, so that we may further enhance the fields of transpersonal psychology and integrative health.

Chapter Forty-Eight

Viewing at a Distance

As previously described, we were able to determine that our sensory systems are continuously fed information because we are sentient. So, what's the best way for sensation-driven beings to handle the stimulus or data the body receives?

The best way is to be clear on *what* we're placing our attention on. To be effective in our practices, we should remember that any information can be processed effectively, impartially, and without prejudices, but in limited amounts, and therefore, it becomes essential for an individual to selectively focus on "relevant stimuli and reject distracting and extraneous ones."

There's information everywhere. Some might be considered noise but knowing what's pertinent takes practice. In remote viewing we choose to not sensor the information that comes in. If we were to delete or disregard it, we might lose crucial information relevant to the target. So, as you focus on delving into the distribution of sensation, perception, and attention, choose to evaluate a target, looking not just at the intra or inner body, but also include evaluating the outer or external world that ebbs and flows around us. We are multidimensional and therefore should consider the multidimensional world we live in and not disregard anything that comes through.

Chapter Forty-Nine

The Emerging God-Human Consciousness: Embracing Oneness

W ould it be fair to say that humans are, by nature, a warring species? As I focused on connecting with the God-source, I initially felt a few things. One was my own lusting after getting my documents finished and turned in, in a timely manner. Another was a sense of calm as I had finally grounded myself, choosing not to judge my lust after a specific outcome. Finally, the answer surfaced. Human beings by nature are a feeling race, empathic, sympathetic, compassionate, and caring. It's our experiences and reactions to life encounters that cultivate aggressiveness or warring-ness. We've been taught how to be unhappy—how to be reactive to others when they don't think, believe, or behave the way we think they should. We've been taught to be happy *'only if'* certain criteria are met. If I get this, then I will be happy. I'll be happy if you trust me; believe in me or feel the same way I do.

We've been experiencing a shift in global consciousness for decades, and lately, it seems to have accelerated. It began over three thousand years ago when, at that time, we were believed to be void of consciousness, unaware of ourselves, our subjective thoughts and feelings, subjective choices, and self-determined interactions with the world around us. We reacted to external stimuli as other animals reacted.

Around the first millennium B.C., our race began functioning much like primates did by mimicking reactions, and around 8000 B.C., we, with our larger, more complex brains, developed a logically coherent language. Humans could speak and were quite intelligent, but were and even today can be unconsciously reactionary.

Humans had functioned by way of an invisible, automatic guidance system void of awareness, but our neurological systems advanced. Humans would soon be guided by audio commands generated from within their own minds, neurological instructions triggered within the right hemisphere of the brain that were transmitted as voices that were heard. Voices were considered to be "of the gods" from the left-brain hemisphere.

As our inner guidance system advanced, the formation of speech carried its own death sentence. Civilizations began to thrive until around 1000 B.C., when those inner voices became confused, opposing, and self-determined, rather than reactionary. As a result, societies began to collapse. Humanity was forced to discover consciousness to survive as the inner voices and external authorities no longer offered adequate guidance.

Author Mark Hamilton suggests that religions are rooted in the unconscious bicameral mind obedient to the voices of external authorities, obedient to the voice of God, gods, rulers, and leaders of the world. The bicameral mind seeks all-knowing truth and automatic guidance from external authorities or authoritarian sources, such as idols, astrologists, gurus, lawyers, psychiatrists, doctors, professors, and journalists.

At one time, our civilization consisted entirely of unconscious, automatic, and reactionary people, and based on their perception of life experiences and their need for survival, they were able to surpass nature to recreate their own consciousness.

Julian Jayne's' book, *Consciousness in the Breakdown of the Bicameral Mind*, sheds light on this shift in consciousness. Two minds now exist within each human being: 1) the mind that seeks guidance from external sources or authorities to make important decisions in times of stress, and 2) the recreated or newly invented conscious mind that bypasses external authorities, providing thoughts and guidance from within one's own mind.

Bicameral thinking functions in concrete terms and in *here-and-now* details, while *conscious thinking* generates an endless collection of subjective perceptions, which allow for even broader understanding and improvements in decision-making. As our consciousness has expanded, it has afforded us the opportunity to see and understand relationships between ourselves and the world around us with more clarity. As the bicameral voices subsided, humans began using religion and prayer to communicate with departed gods. Jayne suggests that humans developed the concept of worship, heaven, demons, angels, sacrifice, divination, exorcism, and the like to evoke guidance from external authorities, namely the gods. Regardless, our shift in consciousness caused an ongoing shift, "from governments of gods, to governments of men, and from divine law to secular law."

Today, most people depend on their automatically deep-rooted mentality alongside external authorities to help them choose or make decisions. Most seek the sure thing instead of using their own innate consciousness or inner wisdom for decision-making.

My purpose for sharing the documented insights and life experiences is to provide evidence that helps you understand just how powerful you are, both in mind and body. This may be terrifying for some, yet others will be ready for a leap into yet another shift of consciousness.

With the knowledge that we are one with God and provided we use the tools we brought into this life, we can surpass outmoded patterns, learned behaviors, and thought forms. The universal design for our consciousness has always been to allow for higher wisdom to take the place of fear, sickness, and treachery. I'll also add that not only are we one with God, but God is a part of all that exists within our realm of consciousness, the God-source is within everything.

War has been perfected and the new challenge is perfecting peace for all living beings. To do so, our species must first find peace within itself to create lasting peace outside itself. It is time for an evolution! Each one of us can do our part by doing our own personal work from the inside (examining our beliefs and experiences, as well as listening to what the body can tell us) and be ready to put all of that good stuff to work outside ourselves. Share what you learn with those you know and love.

It is my belief that when everyone decides to integrate with the God-Human intellect, our world will change for the better. To participate in life at this level creates pure love and compassion, which will become the driving force of a new *super society* known as the *God-Human Civilization*.

In an effort to enlighten you further, I have provided documentation of three cellular memory therapy and remote viewing sessions that may help you understand just what type of information can be harvested when we open ourselves to this emerging quantum consciousness.

RV Target One: *Teenager LB: First introduced by way of a target number through Wayne Carr.*

I viewed the blind target, not knowing what it was, nor did I receive any information that would generate prejudices or preconceived notions. I adopted the protocol from Carr's library rather than my own. I had done one previous session on LB for his parents, and based on the information that came through, they chose to find a school that would provide him with the structure he needed because he became manipulative and domineering at home with his parents and brother.

When I began the second session, I checked in to see how he was doing, but I also held the intention of allowing LB to show me what he needed to rebalance, heal, or succeed in life. His energy suggested that he needed to live in a well-structured environment, have pre-planned meals, and be challenged by educational professionals to show him how to excel in life. During the five-year stretch from 2009 to 2013, LB was placed in a school that was able to provide those things, and he was able to maintain an A/B average. However, he was not living at the school. He returned home each day to a very unstructured and dysfunctional environment.

At the end of June 2014, LB's father called to retain my services once more. Although the family was able to move LB into a school that could challenge and nurture him intellectually, he was still having trouble at home with his mother. Moreover, earlier that month, LB's school structure failed him in that he was hazed by a group of other students because he was seen as different from them. He lost faith in that system and returned home to purchase a rope from the internet. His brother caught him looking for a place to hang himself in his mother's attic. I performed a remote session, and LB's energy suggested that he did not like his appearance, and more especially, he needed to be taught how to progress toward adulthood now that he had reached eighteen years of age. Unfortunately, no family member had been able to offer this guidance and his energy suggested that he was in dire need of a male mentor or a strongly structured program outside the home to aid him in learning how to care for himself and others. To date, the family is in a holding pattern. The father has been in touch with a wilderness camp for troubled teens and LB is not willing to comply.

In many cases, remote viewing sessions offer great insight into specific situations like LB's, but as this case shows, all parties involved have a choice in how they will act out their part. LB had exacted his influence for more than fifteen years and the parents find it difficult to pull in the reigns to regain some control to help create a fully functional, empathic, and benevolent human being.

Even as practitioners use all sensory abilities to aid others and experience a more distinct answer within the session, one must be mindful about maintaining some distance, and allow the chips to fall where they may because it is not our life. Those being viewed may possess the innate ability to use their sentient abilities to reach their highest potential, but without the proper guidance and mentoring, they may lack the fortitude and desire to do so. What they don't know, can't feel, and don't see can sometimes hurt them, as was the case with LB and his family.

Years have passed since LB's remote sessions. He has gone on to college, structured his life and is doing quite well. Graduation is in June.

RV Target Two: *(An abbreviation of the company names is used for remote viewing exercises.) Chac & Ham is using remote viewing for business projects and to assess any and all potential.*

A new business opportunity presented itself and the clients wanted an assessment of their ideas and an analysis of the land they were thinking about purchasing. The session yielded information about both. The property was no good in that it had a large underground water issue and potential investors would cause delays as they moved forward to develop their new model of integrative healthcare. Since the remote viewing session, they have had to make many changes to their model, but they have opened their new facility within an active hospital system but remain autonomous at this time.

RV Target Three: *Carr provided the client's target number with no additional information (blind target only). What can be experienced by a remote viewer when no information is provided prior to starting the session?*

After performing a four-hour evaluation using medical remote viewing protocol, a consultation was performed with the client via telephone to discuss the findings. Much of what he was experiencing was generated by how he felt about his present relationship, but also reflected some bodily damage done during an accident. He had been a professional runner and had to stop for several reasons. During our phone consultation, we discussed options regarding a separation from his spouse. There has been no word back as to how he handled that situation, but he was incredibly happy about the cellular memory work we had done together, which helped him understand why he was experiencing so much body pain. He was touched by the level of connectedness I had with his body—to know so much about his body without knowing who or what the target was before starting the session or ever meeting him in person.

Summary

We, all living things, send and receive information. Each technique explained within the folds of this book can be performed intentionally to communicate or connect with another human or thing, to retrieve physical, mental, emotional, and even spiritual information about that object, to find and retrieve objects connected to another human, or to communicate parapsychologically, allowing one to hear another's thoughts and to empathically feel and understand how another person experiences their life, but even still happens without our conscious will. Developing our specialized sensory structures increases the potential of extracting information from our environment, no matter what environment that might be.

Time after time, CMDT and analysis sessions such as those I use for remote viewing support the notion that physical bodily sensations are codes or distress signals that the cells within our body send out in response to a particular stimulus, such as our thoughts or actions, the result of our mental beliefs, and the emotions we experience at the peak of a specific event. If we focus on the one cause rather than the presenting ailment of any one illness, and if one intentionally looks for that one cause, we will find that it is the accretion of all factors, physical, mental, emotional, spiritual, chemical, and electromagnetic, that will determine the health of the physical form.

All energy, even the smallest forms, can communicate with one another to perform intricate functions, and it stands to reason that we, being of divine consciousness, have the ability to focus our awareness upon any one thing and extract information that will assist the body in reestablishing homeostasis on its own, without external intervention.

If we were to fully embrace our innate abilities and nurture our true gifts, we would not only live healthier lives, but we would also be better able to help individuals take responsibility for their own health and well-being. Wellness begins with education, and we must understand the role of intentionality, thought forms, beliefs, and the emotions we experience. Change your beliefs about not having control over outcomes. Recognize that you have some say in how you want to be treated, how you'll act, what you'll choose, and how you encourage others to adopt a different mindset.

By combining the techniques I've described, humans can reach their highest potential and become one with God to create a new civilization that participates as one cohesive unit for the betterment of all life. If we shift our perspective and realign our consciousness to think in terms of everything being connected to all other things, there is nothing that we cannot achieve.

As societies collapse and rebuild, as they have done since the beginning of time, I believe that it is not only our right, but it is our moral obligation to know ourselves better and take yet another leap forward in our evolution. We have ventured beyond the paranormal and metaphysical and surpassed what we thought we knew about the behavior of the material brain. We now stand on the precipice of a new quantum era. Now, we are better able to *see* and feel the rapture of the heaven-on-earth revolution. This rapture is not a destruction but rather a breaking open or the birth of sorts where we embrace and integrate all that we are.

Imagine, if you will, that instead of referring to heaven as a place that we will rise to after death, we instead see it as shifting through layers of consciousness, much like pulling the petals off a flower. You can even think in terms of walking through new doorways that allow us to transform our negative thought forms to see beyond what is directly in front of our face, use our entire sensory body, and identify deeply with another fellow human. Imagine what the world would be like if everyone had been taught from childhood how to tap into their senses in a much deeper way. A sense of euphoria can be experienced when the cells and energetic body are consciously used to feeling, seeing, hearing, tasting, and smelling beyond their normal senses. We can then use those abilities to enrich our own lives as well as the lives of others.

I intentionally chose to further develop my abilities to aid humanity because I was driven by the God within me. Whether my practices entailed performing individual diagnostic consultations alone or within a formal practicing system or offering group lectures to raise awareness about personal and societal responsibility, I can't help but think that the God within me inspired me to do this work in this manner. The God in me put me here to be of service to others who are ready to make a similar shift in consciousness.

I have dreamt of a day when I would be able to use my abilities to aid individuals in integrating their mind-body skills into all aspects of education and therapeutic practices. To help people exhibit their creativity and innovative approaches. To assist others in moving beyond classical models and disciplines. To emphasize the need for research, practice, and education to effectively and efficiently master their abilities, support self-improvement, and compassionately encourage and inspire change in healthcare.

It has not been my intention to get on my soapbox and tell anyone that they should or should not do as I do. I've instead chosen to share what I have learned from my personal journey and believe that we are each born with innate abilities that, when fostered, transform outmoded paradigms of living, launching us into new paradigms of living that teach others to "value each individual" for their gifts and contributions to humanity that "are of value to everyone and all things." This, I believe, will create more cohesive, intuitive, empathic societies that function within a higher realm of consciousness, portraying the true essence of rapturous living.

As I've developed my abilities, personal friends and associates have suggested that I have an obligation to use my gifts to help others, and yet I beg to differ. I would prefer to think that we've each come here with gifts and abilities that are to be shared. As no two fingerprints are the same, no two people will be the same, nor will they walk, talk, or act the same. We each possess something special that is of value to the world right now, and we each have a right to choose how we will use those special talents to be of service to all our global siblings, no matter the species, race, culture, or religion. I am honored that God felt I was worthy of such gifts, and I would not want to waste one second of my life doing something that did not allow me to feel or understand my fellow God-humans, or His other creatures, more deeply. Living beyond the more well-documented quantum theories into uncharted territory means sometimes "going it alone" in hopes that someday the masses will get to experience the rapture that comes with understanding their own divine God-human nature, as well as their fellow humans, more deeply.

Chapter Fifty

Discovering Brian

In 1989, I moved to Florida and opened a cleaning business. The stress of the move, moving away from my family, and opening a business got to me so I decided to take a meditation class that a business partner told me about. The woman who taught the class looked like the psychic medium in the *Poltergeist* movie played by Zelda Rubinstein. She was robust, confident, sensible, and inviting yet real. After my first class, something happened to me, or perhaps I should say inside me. Whether it was the practice of deep breathing, the quieting of my mind, the realness of the instructor, or the accretion of all factors, a seal of sorts was broken. I was immediately connected to the world in a way that I had never experienced before.

One day after class, the instructor asked me to stay so that we could talk. When all the other attendees left, she quietly pulled an envelope from her desk drawer and asked me to sit on the couch by her side. She slowly handed me the closed, sealed envelope and looked deeply into my eyes. She said, "Nicole, you have a gift and I want to help you nurture it. I believe your gift is so strong that you will be able to do amazing things with it and if you don't do good, you could potentially do very bad things to yourself and others." I felt a deep sigh escape from within me as I think back to that day. She placed her hand on the envelope that now lay in my hands and said, "Please tell me what is in the envelope." With two hands, I began to turn the envelope to the seam to open it. She quickly grabbed my hands and said, "No." That perplexed me. How was I going to tell her what was in the envelope without opening it?

She touched my shoulder softly and reiterated that I possessed an incredible ability and that I would not have to open the envelope to tell her what was in it. She said that if I placed the envelope between my hands and closed my eyes, I would be able to *see* the treasure sealed within. Scared, I jumped from my seat and told her she was crazy. Her voice became deep and forceful with a twinge of urgency vibrating within it. It gave me pause. I sat and did as she asked. As she walked me through the breathing exercises we had done in the meditation classes, I closed my eyes. She said that all I had to do was think of opening myself up to what was coming from within the envelope. I imagined opening my mind. With my physical eyes closed, I somehow opened my inner sight and a window or door into my brain unlocked. It looked as if a black screen had been placed before my brain and colors, objects, and swirling energy took the place of my normal physical eyesight. Still with my eyes closed, a picture began to form within my brain. I could see bright, beautiful, blue eyes, brown curly hair, and dark skin. As I squinted inwardly trying to make sense of what I was seeing, a full face came into clear view. What I saw was a picture of a handsome little boy of about two years of age. Intrigued by what had transpired, I trusted what I saw and shared it with my instructor. She took a deep breath, threw her head back in relief, and smiled as she motioned for me to open the envelope.

I remember opening that envelope very slowly, feeling as if that day, that exact moment, would be one I would never forget. Somehow in the movement of breaking the seal on the envelope, my life would never be the same, and the feeling I had in that instance proved time and time again to be correct.

As the paper crackled between my hands, I closed my eyes, splitting two sides of the paper and reaching in to touch its contents. When firmly in my hand, I opened my eyes and what I saw was nothing short of amazing. It was the exact picture I saw in my mind's eye.

Very matter-of-factly, the instructor said, "Now, tell me where he is." More scared than before, I leaped out of my seat, heading for the door. I told her she was crazy. Not only would I not do it, but I couldn't do it. I am not sure where the fear came from, but for some reason, I felt that a very real threat existed by opening myself up in this way. She reacted to my fear by snatching me by the shirt and forcibly pulling me back to sit down next to her.

My mind raced, making me wonder what the urgency was about, and in that instance, my fear subsided, and my empathy kicked in. She was scared. She was fearful. Not for herself, but for the boy in the picture. Coming to this realization was huge. Something within me understood that this was not about me. It was about the boy, and I could feel that she needed my help. As I experienced my epiphany, she noticed my shift. It felt like my brain had expanded; it was thick but open, deep, malleable, and ready to receive more. Then, something in my body snapped. It was as if all the cells within me came alive. Imagine trillions of cells that look like the Pac-Man men within the

Pac-Man computer game all standing at attention, looking up toward the brain, waiting for further instructions.

The instructor told me that she and a dear friend, who was at that time an ex-CIA agent, were working on a closed missing persons case. This child was two when he disappeared, and it had been eight years since the case went cold. She had tried to communicate with his energy, but she kept hitting a dead end. She went on to say that she knew when we first met that I was to help her and now that I had calmed my own internal chatter, I was ready to learn how to do this.

She had me hold the picture in my hands and go back to my deep breathing. I closed my eyes and the child's face came back into my inner mind's view. I imagined that I was plugging myself into his energy like one would do by plugging a light cord into an electrical box. The child came to life, and it was as if I were inside him. His body lay on the back seat of his fathers' car. As if one, he and I looked up and out of the car window, watching the trees swish by. Our heart was beating slowly, and it felt as if we were getting cold, even though we were wrapped in a blanket. We lay motionless and peaceful, taking in the treetops and road signs as they went by. The car stopped and the father climbed out from behind the wheel. He opened the back door and tugged at the blanket, pulling us into his arms. He carried us for some distance through a wooded area. I could smell the dank soil. The woods were filled with Dogwood trees and the area seemed remarkably familiar to me. In that instant, a memory surfaced that had been stored within the cells of my body.

In the memory, I was a thirteen-year-old child hiking the Virginia woodlands with my dear friend, Evelyn, and her sister, Cindy. Cindy had been doing field research to get her veterinary degree, and Evelyn and I had gone down to help her collect specimens (worms, spiders, and such). My brain linked the smells and the predominant Dogwoods to this exact area. As my cells made the connection, I was transported back to the child being carried by his father. Now, not connected as one, I could walk beside them to take in the environment. As we walked, there were spirits dressed in civil war garb running around and shooting at each other. They were not physically there but energetically tied to this area somehow. I took note and started connecting the dots. Then, a green field filled my mind's eye, and a cartoon character began running through it. That image disappeared shortly after, and a two-by-four piece of wood appeared, and it swung down out of the sky aiming straight for my head. It felt so real that I ducked, and the instructor asked me to describe what I was seeing. I relayed the information, but it made no sense to her, so I went back to what the child was showing me.

An object appeared, which looked like a triangle, then another, which looked like a circle. The circle lay before a small hill and the triangle lay flat on the ground. As if each were communicating with me, the circle formed more circles looping and running back into the hillside. The triangle embedded hundreds more triangles and ran deep into the earth. My brain and cells started piecing the information together, and without consciously helping, the storyline came to life. The green field, the man running in that field of green, and the two-by-four became the name of the area and the mine-Mine Run, Greenwood mine. I made mental notes and went back to paying attention to the data that was streaming in.

I was pulled high into the sky so that I could survey the area. I could see the roadways and how they intersected. A major roadway intersected into a *Y* formation, and the words *Mine Run* and *Paytez*, or *Payne*, floated through my mind. I was drawn then to move back down on the boy and his father. The father placed him on the ground, covered in the blanket, and I watched as the boys' final resting place was dug. I looked back at the boy and his body became an outline of energy. His throat area lit up as if highlighted by a thin, white, vibratory light. I watched helplessly as his energy slipped away. He died that day, laying there in the dank, dark soil with spirits from the civil war re-enacting a deadly power struggle. There was a sense of resolve emanating from him; his father didn't love him and there was nothing he could do to change that.

I stood quickly as the information coursed through my veins and walked to the door. My instructor asked me where I was going and with an urgent goodbye, I hollered back over my shoulder, "I will be back. I have got to go look for something."

Not really sure where I was going or what I was looking for, I got into my car and sped off in search of a local library. I found one between my instructor's home and my own. As I walked through the door, something told me to use the computer to plug in some of the information I had received: Dogwood trees of Virginia, Mine Run, Greenwood mine, military bases of Virginia, and Wars of Virginia. I wrote down the ID numbers of the books they had listed under those topics and went to work finding them on the library shelves. I soon found a table to begin thumbing through page after page, still not clear on what I was looking for. I found many things that fit, so I began making copies of the pages so that I could take them home to marinate and meditate on what had been handed to me. I remember feeling a bit overwhelmed, exhilarated, and yet beaten when I reached the end of the last book on the table.

There it was. A sign! Something I could not dismiss. It felt like the universe was calling me out. *MINERAL RESOURCES, Virginia*, it read in black print with its address and phone number clearly listed, as if it were in very dark, bold print jumping off of the page.

I wrote it down on one of my copies and headed home. Once settled back in, I pulled the number and chose not to wait. I dialed the number. The phone rang, and a very deep, masculine voice answered. "Good afternoon, Division of Geology and Mineral Resources. This is Michael Upchurch."

I took a deep breath and began. "Hello, Michael. My name is Nicole, and this is going to be a very odd conversation. If you bear with me, I will explain."

His voice softened and sounded as if he had the patience of a saint. "Sure. How can I help you?"

"Well, Michael, I have recently been introduced to the world of psychic phenomenon, and my mentor-slash-instructor involved me in a missing persons case where a child had disappeared eight years ago. I have never done this sort of thing before, and quite frankly, I am searching for proof that I did, in fact, make contact with a missing child, one I have never met or been up close or personal with. As my instructor guided me into what seemed a trance-like state, I saw some things in my mind's eye. I don't know if you believe in this sort of thing, but I hope you can help me. Would you mind if I shared what I saw, and could you tell me whether these places exist or not?"

"Yes Nicole, and I have just the thing that can help us. It's a computer that links me to the entire area. As you tell me what you saw, I can plug in words, and we will see what comes up."

I ran through all I had seen while being connected to the missing child and Michael's computer proved to be a Godsend.

"Nicole, we have a Mine Run, and we have two Greenwood mines. One runs back into a hillside and the other runs straight down into the earth."

I am sure you can imagine my surprise. "I saw the spirits of men running around hiding behind trees and rocks, shooting at one another. Did a war or battle take place there?"

"Yes, one took place nearby."

"Is there a military base nearby? As the child and I were linked together, I could hear planes flying overhead and knew by the sounds that they were not normal commercial planes. They sounded like heavy military planes."

"Yes, there is," he said.

"Michael, are there any maps of the area and if so, can I get one?"

"Sure, I can actually blow up the maps, print them out, and FedEx them overnight to you so that you and your people have them in the morning, Nicole."

I thanked him for listening and for his willingness to help and we hung up.

This experience rocked my world. I was amazed at the clarity of the information and still even more amazed that Michael could tap into a computer that would provide us with proof that this place existed. I had never physically been to the location where the child took me, but I had been to the Virginia woodlands hiking and collecting bugs and worms. The place was stored within the cells of my body right down to the smell of the soil and the genre of trees that were prevalent in that specific area. What would have happened had I doubted any of those things I had seen and experienced?

As promised, the maps were delivered the following morning. I opened the package and found a number of maps inside, each with the area in question, yet each map was blown up bigger to get us closer to the mine and the roadway that the father drove to bury his son in a secluded spot. I circled the spot between the road and the Greenwood mine that ran straight down into the earth, bound the maps with rubber bands, and drove to my instructor's home.

My heart was racing as I knocked on her door. She opened it and smiled. "I was wondering what happened to you. Where did you go when you left here?"

I told her I went to the library to look up the things the child was showing me.

"Well, did you find anything?" she asked.

I handed her the maps.

"What is this?"

"Maps! I circled the exact location that the child took me to." She opened the maps on the kitchen table, and I pointed to where the circle was.

"How did you do this?" she asked.

"After a few hours of searching the library books, I stumbled on the last page of one that had the name and number for Mineral Resources in Virginia. So, I called the number and spoke to the man there. I told him what I saw, and he used his computer to see if the place was real. I am sure you can imagine how scared I was to call the number and how amazed I was to find out that the place with all the descriptors was real." She hugged me and told me that it was important that I use my newfound gift to do good things. She warned me; should I consider using the gift to do terrible things, it would boomerang back and adversely affect me tenfold.

That was the beginning of an amazing journey. Each technique I learned, each client I worked on, and each project I engaged in allowed me to practice and hone my skills. With practice, I gained more confidence and I found new and better ways of managing my abilities and doing incredible things. Interestingly, you don't have to have first-hand knowledge or an education in a particular field to trust the information that comes through intuitively. I have found it just as easy to trust the information that comes through and use the internet or an encyclopedia to confirm it as true. By being open and willing, the universe conspires to help us and we attract more data. Being the detective and doing our follow-up research on specific words is easy.

I had never searched the internet to confirm or verify that there had been a war or scuffle in the area of Virginia that the missing boy's energy showed me. Today, while writing about this experience, I happened upon it when I was looking up the information about Mineral Resources.

The Mine Run Campaign, The Battle of Mine Run ran from November 27th through December 2nd of 1863 in Orange County Virginia with an inconclusive outcome between Commanders Major General George Meade of the Army of the Potomac and General Robert E, Lee of the Army of Northern Virginia. Finding that information now just reinforces my trust in the universe and how it and I communicate with one another. It simply amazes me, even now after so many years and so, so many experiences.

I have heard other intuitive people talk about how their gifts were revealed to them only after they had suffered a near-death experience or physical trauma. I had many traumatic experiences throughout my life, although I don't believe we have to suffer traumas to get in touch with this side of ourselves. When working with clients and their children, I can teach them in minutes what took me years to learn on my own. Everyone is empathic to a certain degree. Everyone is born with extra sensory abilities, although during rearing, many children are not taught to develop them. Most adults don't know that the brain of a child is malleable and that they are capable of absorbing mass amounts of information. With purposeful practice, using intuitive abilities becomes second nature, an acquired behavior or trait. If we learn to trust what we sense at an early age, we can not only obviate or prevent illness, accidents, and trauma, but we can also learn to live life more fully engaged, awake, and in acceptance of the extraordinary power we all possess.

Fact is, anyone can do the things I have done. You can prevent or alleviate trauma. WE ARE HUMAN, and often, trauma can be the precursor to evolution so that we do not stagnate, or so that we don't wipe ourselves from the face of the Earth. The ontogeny of human development was not gradual; it was spontaneous like The Big Bang. Yet, we develop, babies develop, and we all evolve in our practices. Before anyone can use it at will, choosing how we will practice can be important. Then, we practice and keep practicing, until it (the practice) just becomes one with who we are.

A New Reality ~ Accelerating Human Potential

We are at a tipping point in history, abounded with opportunities, where you get to decide how you want to live your life. You can dwell on the past, your experiences, and perceptions, and let your emotions rule, or you can embrace this new reality, where you realize that you are more powerful and more connected than ever before. As we integrate the puzzle pieces that have been discussed throughout this book, we are closer to understanding the truth about what kind of power we possess. Listening more deeply and learning to trust your intuition, and not fighting it, *it* becomes as natural as breathing without thinking about it. By listening to our intuition, we're not only able to continuously avoid traumas, but we can also remain open and constantly stream any energy that's coming and going through our own energetic field. It's when we forget our connectedness—when we forget to listen—that we fall out of balance and out of the natural flow of life.

So, how do we do it? How do we trust the information that streams in from all outside sources? Think back to the Shogi study in one of my opening chapters where I shared how the caudate nucleus within the basal ganglia of the brain is responsible for our intuitions. I have found that the key to receiving pure information is related to '*what we focus on.*'

For the cortex—or basal ganglia—to detect something, either we or the intelligence within us needs to decide what it is we or it is to focus on. Doing so will allow us to fundamentally become one with whatever we focus our attention on.

Sensory Discipline and Intuition Mastery

Learning how to use your innate sensory abilities can be an adventure. There is always a beginning; a place where it's exciting when the smallest successes happen almost out of the blue and almost knock you off your feet, a middle; where you practice your heart out until you feel like you're so sensitive that you have to hide from all of the toxicity in the world, then levels off after a brilliant crescendo; bringing you to rest and at ease into a state of peaceful wonder. I remember all three stages of development. I loved how exciting it was to learn new things in the beginning. The meat of my development; the second stage of my intuitive development was quite difficult in that I found myself to be sensitive to food, water, toxic chemicals, EMFs, loud noises, spirit activity and anything else that did not come from inside of myself. I wanted to run from anything that stressed my senses. As my abilities peaked in the third stage, using my senses to sift through and stream data was so easy I thought I might be doing something wrong. Upon further introspection, I realized that there was an old mental tape running rampant in my unconscious mind telling me that I would always have to work hard for what I wanted. When I broke through into stage three a new factual story began to play out in my life. The more open I remained, the less I struggled. I had to choose to let go, to disassociate from my old self and embrace the new.

Whether you've read this as a beginner or a master, you are truly capable of magical works. Always remember that breathwork, focus, and intention will be the keys to unlocking the genius that lives within you, low-level emotions will bring low-level experiences and, if you can imagine something bigger and better, you can create new and amazing experiences.

To this end, this closing chapter is for you, the one who's ready to commit to personal growth, sensory proficiency, and purposeful living.

Personal Development & Self-Empowerment

Having a willing partner to work with will enhance your experiences as you learn but it is not essential. You can practice many of these techniques on your own, just remember that breathwork opens all of your energy centers and makes each of these techniques much more effective.

Mastery and the power of touch ~ Psychometry

Practice 1: Communing with nature

Find a beautiful tree to lean up against. Rest back onto the trunk. Close your eyes and lay your hands on its base or root system. Provided you've inhaled and exhaled deeply, three or four times, hold only one request in your mind. SHOW ME.

You will not send your energy into that tree but instead imagine as you think the words 'show me', that you've granted the tree permission to send its energy to you. I liken the experience to sticking a plug into a power outlet. You're plugging into the tree and by doing so, the tree sends you energy that will bring images, sensations, and ultimately an innate understanding of what it thinks, feels, believes and how it experiences its own life. Keep a notepad and journal. Each time you practice the technique you'll deepen your relationship with the tree. As the tree learns to trust you, you'll be able to ask more complex questions.

Practice 2: Touching objects that belong to others to see what they see, feel what they feel, and walk in their shoes.

With permission from the owner of an object (keys, rings, watches, clothing, etc.), you will start with your breathwork to ground yourself. Then place the chosen object between your hands, (your dominant hand atop the other). Focus your awareness on the space just above your eyebrows and imagine that it looks like a darkened television screen. When you can see the television screen in your minds-eye, imagine that your energy plugs into the object that you're holding in your hands. Use the words SHOW ME as if you are speaking to a living breathing being. Further imagine that the object in your hands begins to send information, pictures, and past experiences related to the owner of the object into your minds-eye. Let the images, feelings and information come.

Write it all down, and please keep in mind that the information that comes through is about the object or the owner of the object, not about you. You are merely allowing your body to become a vessel that can catch and release whatever information that object decides to share with you.

Practice 3: Using touch to experience the life of a human or animal. In this instance I would suggest that you request permission before starting your practice. I practiced on animals as a young child and progressed into using psychometry to diagnose racecars. That then organically led to humans to help analyze the issues they were experiencing. Practicing with humans should only be started after working with plants, objects, and animals. It is too easy to lose yourself when you allow yourself to take in the energy of another person.

Echolocation, Empathy & Telepathy

Find someone who is willing to practice with you. You'll be exercising a part of your brain that you probably haven't purposefully used before. Don't be surprised if after a few tries you notice a slight headache. With practice that sensation will pass.

Practice 1: Have your partner draw a series of stick figures. Ask them to choose one, and only one of them but tell them not to tell you what they are thinking. Do not look at them. Look only at their artwork and survey the energy that emanates from the paper. SEE if anything they have drawn sticks out. Then, close your eyes. Ask the artist/practice partner to send a thought of the stick figure they choose but not to speak their choice aloud. Remember that you are catching their thoughts either through echo-like signals, images, or feelings related to what a particular figurine is acting out in the picture. Did your partner's thought echo off the page, did they draw it so perfectly in their mind that you could see it in your mind's eye with little effort, or could you feel your partner's emotional attachment to whatever the stick figurine was acting out? For example: was the stick figure catching a fish, energetically running up a hill, performing a peaceful yoga pose, or playing a game of football? When someone sends thoughts to you, don't discount their emotional attachment to whatever they're sending.

Practice 2: Sit with your favorite pet. Talk to them first as you ask them to sit with you. If they are resistant, you will have to take time to gain their trust. Do not force them to sit, as this will cause a disconnect and they won't allow you to connect. If the animal willingly rests near you, softly place your hand or hands on it. Do your breathwork to balance your energy. If your energy is bad or your emotions are negative in nature you will traumatize the animal. You don't want that.

Breathe. Then in your mind say those magic words, SHOW ME. Rest, breathe, and close your eyes. Focus on that blank TV screen just above your eyebrows. When a picture of that animal forms in your minds-eye without you forcing it to happen, you have mind-melded with that animal. This type of connection can never be broken. This connection is forever, so no matter where you go, when that animal thinks of you, or you think of it, you will both know at lightning speed.

When you get proficient at these practices, you can use the same technique with humans, but a word to the wise...knowing your own energy, thoughts, beliefs and emotions first is crucial. You can lose yourself if you're not careful.

You can also incorporate touch/psychometry into this practice if you cannot connect via thought in the beginning. Using touch expedites the energy transfer. As you practice more often it will get easier to connect without touching anything or anyone. Remember thought travels faster than light. Some people are powerful thinkers, some are very tender or docile in thought.

Cellular memory detoxification-self therapy

For charts and key points that will help you to ask your body better questions, refer back to Chapter 45 on how this technique works otherwise consider this to be a reminder.

Use your visualization techniques when speaking to their body. I mentioned that I tend to use a symbol such as a house to represent my body or I will skip the house and move straight to the cells to ask questions if an ache or pain presents itself.

Practice visualization: Focus on your breathing. Once you achieve the body breath balance you can imagine or visualize that you are standing on your front doorstep. Reach for your doorknob, open it and enter. Take note of what you see as you enter. Is the house in disarray? Is it a distinct color? Is it decorated differently? Does this inner house look different from the house in which you physically live? If so, is your body trying to tell you that it would prefer this house over the one you actually reside in? Pay attention to what you see.

Once you are inside, look for the person in charge of running the household. (I tend to look for the aspect of myself, since she is the one that handles all of my organ and system operations). As you enter the house, you can simply holler or whisper your own name and request a response.

It sounds a bit like this; "Nikki, hello...where are you?"

She answers, "I'm upstairs in the bedroom."

So, I head upstairs to the bedroom to see what she's doing.

Take note as to how that Source energy reveals itself to you, also take note of what it's doing as you enter the room. You can even ask your Source what it's doing if it is not obvious. Have a conversation with it. Tell it how much you would enjoy the two of you working together and ask it if it wants your help. Once you two make friends you can ask your Source if it's willing to talk to you about organ and system functions, business affairs or even personal issues.

You can use the rooms of your house to symbolize organs within your body. (e.g., water in the bathtub may symbolize heavy emotions held within the bladder; a broken thermostat may be symbolic of your own inner thermometer being off kilter due to an infection or illness; the cellar may symbolize your reproductive or pelvic cavity; the attic may represent your brain, and so on...) As your Source guides you through your rooms pointing out specific trinkets, furniture or fixtures, you can ask the Source exactly what organ the object represents. You can look for bumps, bruises, scratches. You can even taste and smell things or feel the texture of your organs. You will use all of your senses while working with your Source. Your Source may use whatever symbols are necessary in order to help you understand what it has been feeling and how a particular emotion affects that specific organ. You may find a few different emotions in an organ and, you may also find the same emotion residing within more than one organ. Understand that there are many forms of each emotion and there will be many memories connected to those emotions; whatever they may be.

Let's go back to the bedroom and talk to Nikki so that you can better understand just how in-depth you can get with the questioning process.

***

Nikki is sitting at her desk working on some papers as I enter the bedroom. So I ask, "What are you working on?"

Nikki: "You know... we're writing a book."

Me: Yes, I know, and I was trying to help our readers better understand how this cellular memory process works.
Nikki: "Oh, okay. Sorry."

Me: "No problem. So, we're drafting a book?"

Nikki: "Yes."

Me: "Can I take you away from your writing to talk for a moment about our body?"

Nikki: "Sure!"

Me: "Are there any areas of the body that are in need of attention today?"

Nikki: "Always!" (She gives me a sheepish grin.)

Me: "You're so funny! Okay, so what organ wants to speak to me today?"

Nikki: "The liver."

Me: "Is this imbalance emotional or physical in nature?"

Nikki: "Emotional."

Me: "What emotion resides here?"

Nikki: "Hatred."

Me: "Interesting... I have never hated anything... hmm... Show me the very first memory you have of this emotion of hatred."

Nikki shows me a filmstrip-like memory of the dog I used to play with as a child. "You remember, the one that was hit by a car and her owner shot her?"

Me: "Nikki, I understand the link between hatred and the memory, but why would this show up now within my liver?"

Nikki: "Yesterday you took your dog companion, Kiawa, to the animal shelter to be cremated. You know how much you love her, and you were thinking about how cruel people can be to animals. You had previously worked at an animal shelter and you were aware of what you would see when you visited this one. You and your friends walked around to look at the dogs that were being held in the pens for adoption. The police officer told you that eighty dogs and cats were being euthanized per week. There were so many unwanted, mistreated animals. Seeing the dirty, frail, lonely creatures cramped into those small runs brought up the feelings you had about your dog friend being chained to her doghouse. You could feel their pain and sadness. It made you feel that hatred all over again. Your liver is trying to detoxify those feelings so that you can live in a state of love. Hatred has no home in this body. It must go.

Me: "I am at a loss and feel as if I should do something. What can I do to stop the atrocities that are done to animals? And... if I can't do anything to stop it, what can I do to help my liver feel better?"

Nikki: "Tell the truth, just as you experience it."

Me: "The truth about what? I don't think I understand what you're alluding to."

Nikki: "The truth about how animals also use extrasensory perception to communicate with us. The truth about how we are all connected. We are all energy. Harmony, respect, and compassion are to be our main focus from here forward."

Me, judging what I heard my body say sounded like this: "Oh, you're opening a can of worms. Do we really need to go there?

So, you see, we tend to judge what we hear, even when it comes from within.

Instead of accepting what my source just told me, I chose to be judgmental. I chose to make up my own agenda rather than to listen and breathe. Take a look at her response to my criticism.

Nikki: "I don't think you will get to choose when it will be revealed. There are events that will take place on this planet that will align you with the proper time and place to share these truths. All you have to do is hold the intention and be who you are. I will help you when the time comes."

Without judgment or criticism I responded, "I know and trust that you will."

You can have conversations just as you would with a friend. You just have to pay attention to what you see, smell, taste, hear and feel. We were given these sensory gifts for a reason. Trust your Source to guide you to the truth of a matter. Know that whatever route you choose to take in order to tap into your Source energy, really doesn't matter. Whatever vehicle you use to "get there" will work, just as long as you get there. The key is in your awareness and intention. What do you intend to accomplish by going within? Be clear on your intent. For me, it is about maintaining homeostasis. Staying balanced so that illness does not manifest, and if by chance it does, it won't stay long because I am ever present in my awareness.

So, let's look again at the process of communication.

Once you get inside and know that you have contacted your Source, you ask it to identify the organ or system that needs attention. Then you ask it to show you what emotion is connected to that organ.

Once you hear what it tells you, you ask your Source to show you the memory connected to that emotion. Now... you can either ask to see the memory or you can ask it to take you to the very first memory it has of ever feeling that particular emotion. There really is a difference between the two.

Remember Key point number eight: We ask the Source to show us the very first memory (the trigger memory) it has stored within that organ in order to see just when that emotion was anchored. If we find the anchor memory and give it our full attention first, all other memories will fall like dominos. The body will then be able to achieve balance easily, effortlessly, and typically, more quickly. If you choose to start with just any ole' memory it may take you longer to regain inner balance. Be mindful that there are many forms of each emotion stored within our bodies. There are many experiences that your Source will want to share with you. Speaking from personal experience, I have found it easier to go directly to the issue that started all the trouble in the first place. By paying attention to that one first, all others will just show up for viewing and not wreak havoc on your emotional state. You should be able to view them with little attachment.

Remote viewing – Develop the ability to SEE, Everything Everywhere, Always

Special thanks to Dr. Carr for graciously granting permission, allowing me to share the information compiled for the instruction of the basic remote viewing process—a free version—which beginners, or non-psychics, as well as advanced psychics, can get familiar with in five minutes and perform a session within five to ten minutes.

This game, as Carr referred to it, was set up to sharpen viewing or psychic skills in a way that allows you to get constant feedback on many targets at once in a fun way. Carr suggests that if you have fun with it in a carefree manner, you'll achieve much better results. He also suggests that you think of it as a form of meditation.

The game can be played alone or with another person, by phone, or as a group in preparation for workshops or a home study program.

Sensory Skill Set Development – Learning to remote view and the basic remote viewing process is provided for you in the closing chapter.

Basic remote viewing process: How to Play

Two people face each other, one with a target (e.g., a photo of an object), and the other remote views that target for five to ten minutes. During the process, the viewer verbalizes their impressions of the target, while the monitor gives feedback on the impressions. The target is then revealed. The two people then switch roles and do another target. (If done solo, there is no feedback until the target is revealed.)

STEP ONE: CREATE A TARGET POOL

This is the quick-start option for those who do not want to wait to create a larger target pool.

PAIRED OPTION (REQUIRES TWO PEOPLE): To play immediately: (1) You can just think of a target without writing it down OR (2) think of one target and write it down on a piece of paper OR (3) cut a photo of a target out of a magazine or use a postcard or another discrete photo. You intend for that target you selected to be viewed by the other person. You do not tell the other person what the target is. The other person can either be present or on the phone.

SOLO OPTION (REQUIRES ONLY ONE PERSON): (1) Think of at least three targets and write them down on separate sheets of uniform 8.5 x 11 blank paper OR (2) cut at least three photos of a target out of a magazine or use postcards or other discrete photos. Place each photo or sheet in a separate opaque folder. Shuffle the folders up so you don't know which is which. Then, blindly pull out one of the folders as your current target and place it next to you. Place the other target folders ten feet or more away from you.

THE REGULAR, NON-QUICK-START OPTION (CAN BE DONE SOLO OR WITH TWO PEOPLE): Two people are recommended for the best, most rapid learning. Get ten to forty targets by cutting pages out of magazines like National Geographic, or by going to some travel sites on the Internet and printing out photos of targets. You can also go to a search engine. If you're in a hurry, you can forgo the photos and just print the name of each target on separate sheets of paper. This will work but not quite as well as photos.

Target photos should be discrete landmarks, events, or people that you can point at, as if you were there. Example targets include a photo of the Eiffel Tower, Mt. Everest, a dance contest, a person swimming, a buffalo, and so on. Avoid abstract or vague targets (e.g., a stock market crash).

You can also find the section called "Ideal Target Characteristics" on the web pages provided on the Internet.

If you cut the target out of a magazine, cross out what is on the other side of the page. Even then, it is still possible, although not likely for the viewer to view what is on the back side or get a blend of front and back. It is a little better (not crucial) to make a color photocopy of the side of the page you want as the target, so that the back side of the final target page is blank.

It is also better if more than one person contributes to the target pool. Do not show the targets you have put in the pool to anyone and do not look at any targets that anyone else has added to the pool.

Targets are then shuffled and kept in an opaque folder.

STEP TWO: PAIR OFF

SOLO OPTION (NO PAIRING OFF): Place the target by first blindly selecting a target by closing your eyes and picking from a shuffled pile or folder containing the targets on a cleared table near you. Follow the instructions for the actual session.

PHONE OPTION: You can also do these procedures by phone without sitting and facing each other.

<u>REGULAR OPTION</u>: Pair off with someone and sit facing each other. It's a little better if there is a small table in between so that the viewer can write or draw. Have a pen and some blank paper on the table. Make sure both parties have read all the instructions given here.

Choose which person will first be the monitor and which person will first be the viewer. The monitor takes the target file and looks at the top target only. The monitor intends that target to be the current target and studies it for a moment. The monitor does not try to telepathically send the image, rather he or she just intends the current target. The viewer's intention is that the top target that he or she is looking at is the current target to be viewed by the viewer.

During this time, the viewer sits for thirty to sixty seconds to let their mind clear and to intend to view the current target.

STEP THREE: Actual session takes five to ten minutes

A) THE VIEWER'S ROLE: REPORTING IMPRESSIONS AND STATING "analytic overlays".

<u>SOLO OPTION:</u> The viewer is to follow the non-solo instructions by stating aloud the impressions that come to them. The only difference is that you won't be getting feedback from a partner.

The solo meditation option: You may also try doing the session as a meditation (e.g., with legs crossed, eyes closed, straight back, aware of your breathing, mind quieted, and placing gentle intention on moving to the target).

REGULAR OPTION: As the viewer faces the monitor with eyes open, the viewer intends to receive impressions about the current target. These impressions are faint, brief sensory impressions of taste, smell, temperature, color, sound, texture, luminescence, shape, and so on. Keep thinking in terms of the five senses, as if you had a mental checklist. You don't want to leave any senses unattended. (The viewer can, at times, experiment doing it with their eyes closed.)

The viewer can also get impressions of height, weight, size, and shape, as well as impressions of energy and emotionality. The viewer can also report impressions of basic concepts, such as human-made, natural, historical, intelligent, and so on.

The viewer can also get impressions of what are called physicals. Physicals are basic, elemental, generic, open-ended things that are made of atoms, such as land, water, structures, stones, vegetation, people, animals, beings, mountains, sky, ice, and so on.

All these impressions last from one-sixth of a second to two seconds. They are fleeting, fragmentary, evaporative, sensory-based, and they don't always make sense. Don't try to make sense of them.

As these sensory-based impressions arise, one at a time, the viewer reports them aloud to the monitor. The viewer may say things such as salty, blue, narrow, whooshing, flowing, rocks, land, red, structure, person, rough, circular, old, hot, cold, moving, sweet, vegetation, earthy, and so on.

All these kinds of vague impressions or data are called low-level data. The viewer states these impressions (low-level data) aloud to the monitor, and the monitor responds to each one individually (see next section).

The viewer does not censor anything. The viewer does not do any detective work or try in any way to figure out what the target is. Do not accumulate data. The role of the viewer is just to <u>report</u> what they got and nothing more. The viewer never attempts to guess what the target is. They don't care if they are right. The viewer tries to get a flow of impressions going; (e.g., one impression every two to four seconds). Your personal flow will vary but try to let one impression come after the other. Verbalize them aloud as you get them. Try to be more like a bloodhound than like Sherlock Holmes.

Think of yourself as an unbiased reporter of impressions and nothing more.

If nothing comes to you, no big deal!

1. Just let your mind go blank for a while and breathe.

AND/OR consider playfully allowing information to come. Don't pressure yourself to be perfect.

2. Some remote viewers suggest that in practice you just arbitrarily make up stuff out of the blue. (Fake it until you make it so to speak.) If you are <u>resistant</u> to being arbitrary and contrived, then you need to examine your own resistances. Consider what is triggering your resistance to being completely arbitrary. Are you hanging on to a belief about how you or the process should be? If you are capable of saying

words, you are capable of being arbitrary. It's that simple, so, don't complicate it; just try.

OPTIONAL ADDITIONAL WAYS OF GETTING IMPRESSIONS OF THE TARGET:

The viewer can also QUICKLY:

1. Do little scribbles of shapes or do quick sketches of impressions that come to mind.

2. Use your hands and arms to reach out and touch the target, as well as feel and trace its basic shape, texture, and energy with your hands. Feel the target kinesthetically. Stand up and let your body move like the target; step into the target and move.

3. Probe the sketches with your pen or fingers for more impressions.

4. Report these impressions aloud to the monitor as you get them.

VIEWER ALSO DECLARES ALL AOLs, LABELS, OR HIGH-LEVEL DATA DURING THE SESSION:

During the session, some of the impressions that the viewers get will remind them of something that they recognize (e.g., a submarine). What happens is that as the viewer gets faint impressions, their mind will automatically fan through a mental Rolodex of recognizable images and memories to find a memory that matches all or some of the vague impressions they are getting. They will then automatically produce a label that makes sense of what they might be viewing.

For example, the Eiffel Tower, the Pyramids of Giza, and The eruption of Mt. St Helen's are all labels of specific things we can recognize. On the other hand, words like "high" or "salty" or "blue" are sensory impressions, not labels. Labels are also referred to as AOL, which stands for analytic overlay. This process occurs automatically; however, it is not to be encouraged or deliberately done. No deliberate energy investment goes into this process except to declare and let go.

Any of this data that is a specific label (or a mental Rolodex memory match) and that is not vague or open-ended is called high-level data. For example, Stonehenge is high-level data, whereas words like large, ancient, gray, stone, blocks, green, land, hills, and circular are its low-level equivalence.

When the viewer gets an AOL, he or she should verbalize it aloud with the intention of declaring it and letting it go. The viewer then continues attending to and stating his vague sensory (low-level) impressions in the role of a reporter. The viewer lets go of high-level data and always attends to the low-level data. It's always a temptation to hold on to an AOL, but don't give in to that temptation.

When the viewer declares and releases the AOLs, they will say out loud things like: "AOL - Eiffel Tower" or "AOL - Mt Rushmore" or "AOL - Stonehenge." The monitor does not respond in any way to the AOLs, but just remains silent. The viewer can also say, "Deduction - Eiffel Tower" or "Reminds me of Eiffel Tower" if they prefer (as long as they let it go afterward).

3B) THE MONITOR'S ROLE: GIVING FEEDBACK

The monitor gives feedback for each impression as the viewer verbalizes them.

If the impression is in the target, the monitor says, "Check" (correct). If the impression is definitely not in the target, the viewer remains silent.

If it's plausible that the impression is in the target, the monitor says, "Plausible." If the impression is in the target, not literally but in a sense, the monitor says, "In a sense," or "Partly." If the viewer doesn't know if the impression is in the target, then the monitor says, "Unknown."

Remember that the picture is not the target. The picture only represents the target. The actual target is the actual structure, object, area, place, person, or event. The picture is only a small sample from one point of view of the actual target. For example, if "sky" or "water" is not in the picture but obviously there in the target, then it is part of the target.

STEP FOUR: THE MONITOR BEGINS CUING, OR GIVES "MOVEMENT EXERCISES" (Lasts half of the five-to-ten-minute session)

In the last half of the session, if the monitor hears the viewer say something that really feels like it's completely on target, the viewer can say something like, "Go with that."

The monitor can look at the target picture and determine what the major aspects of the target are. For example, major aspects could be people, structures, energies, color, smell, taste, or activity. The monitor can then say things like, "Cue on activity," or "What smells do you perceive?" The viewer then, in turn, attends to smell or activity and states their vague sensory impressions (and continues to declare and let go of AOLs).

The monitor can also say things like, "Move twenty-five feet above the target and describe" or "Move directly in front of the target and describe." The viewer then attends to these instructions and states their vague sensory impressions (and continues to declare and let go of AOLs).

STEP FIVE: FINAL SKETCH AND SUMMARY

QUICK START OPTION: Let the sketch be optional.

REGULAR OPTION: In the last eighth of the session, the viewer sketches the target trying to capture the basic shape, energy, and feeling. It is better to draw a vague, open-ended sketch instead of something specific that you recognize. Try to feel all around the page as you sketch to discover what shapes want to be drawn. Declare and let go of AOLs during this process.

The viewer can then spend thirty to sixty seconds probing various parts of their sketch with their pen and writing down any vague impressions they get from the probe, right in the sketch at the location where they probed.

Finally, the viewer gives a brief summary of what information they received by using sensory-based, low-level language only. For example: "I picked up something that seems outdoors, round, warm, liquid, or watery, surrounded by vegetation. It smelled earthy and fresh. I heard gurgling sounds. There seem to be animals or people present."

STEP SIX: THE MONITOR REVEALS THE TARGET (Final Feedback)

At this point, the monitor shows (or states) the target to the viewer without revealing any of the other targets in the folder to him or herself or to the viewer. Let the viewer study the photo of the target for as long as he or she wants to. Point out the similarities between the sketches, summary, and the targets. Notice "what" in the photo triggered the AOLs. Notice if shapes, contours, sections, or patterns in the sketch resemble the photo. Don't expect to totally nail the target! Look at what you did get. What the viewer thought the target was is not important. What is important is that the viewer describes the target, even if he or she is clueless about what it actually was. Don't be too perfectionistic or judgmental. Be honestly objective.

STEP SEVEN: SWITCH WITH YOUR PARTNER. The monitor now becomes the viewer, and the viewer becomes the monitor. The new monitor takes the old target in the folder and places it on the bottom of the pile.

The process of viewing is repeated for the next target for another five-to-ten-minute session. The pair can continue to switch every five to ten minutes until they decide to quit. (Try six in a row, three per person.)

VARIATIONS OF THE GAME:

Besides trying the quick start, by phone, solo, and meditation options, you can also vary the session time by trying two-to-three-minute sessions or fifteen-minute sessions doing the same process.

You can also try it in a group where there is one monitor, and the rest of the group simultaneously verbalizes their impressions out loud to the single monitor. Also, everyone in the group can pair off into viewers and monitors and do targets simultaneously.

Experiment with your own variations and have fun with it. Notice how it gets you in touch with your intuitive side, and how you begin to trust yourself more and more.

(Free training provided by Wayne Carr)

Tutorial Game template:

Mind-melding, telepathy, energy-thought transfer

Step one: Choose five or six objects from around any room in your home or office and place them on the table. Be sure to choose objects that do not look similar in nature (e.g., a brown plate, silver fork, white cup with writing on it, an orange candle that smells like tangerines and cloves, a block of cheese, a green apple sliced, etc.). Each is different in color, size, shape, texture, smell, and taste.

Step two: Deep breathing exercise. Ask your child or student to breathe with you. Take in a deep breath until you cannot fill your lungs with any more air. Hold for three seconds, then exhale out of your mouth until your lungs are totally empty. Repeat this process three or four times until you begin to feel a bit dizzy. (If you do feel dizzy, use this time to imagine or visualize that you are a tree, rooting yourself deep into the earth.) Once you have done your breathing exercise, the sender and receiver will survey all the objects chosen for this game. As the sender surveys the objects, the sender will choose only one object to hold in mind without fixating with the eyes on that object. Once the sender has the object firmly in mind, the sender will send the thought or image to the person in the receiving position. As the sender transmits the thought of the object, they should send the image in different ways (e.g., type-written letters, as the object itself, drawn as if drawing it on a pad with colored pencils, painting it, or imagining taking a bite out of it if the object being thought of is food). If the receiver is open and receptive, the object will come to mind very quickly. (It is important for the sender to remember to tell the receiver not to doubt what comes through. Just report what comes into their mind's eye, as well as any sensations they feel, taste, smell or hear.) Repeat the exercise by switching positions. If you were the sender, you would then become the receiver, and so on. Practice until the exercise becomes effortless, and always delete any objects once the receiver is correct. Add in new objects as you go. If you are working with a child, keep the game short and always remember high praise gets them excited about playing the game more often. I believe as Fulton does; children should be trained at the earliest possible age to familiarize themselves with the potential of echolocation so that the malleability of their brain can be engaged to magnify their inherent capabilities.

One last bit of advice for the worry warts and card-carrying empaths of the world. Don't fear what is to come. Life is forever evolving. The carbon-based bio suits we wear, or the body avatar our spirit commands during this lifetime was never made to be permanent. At our core, we are pure energy that never dies and only changes form upon the death of the physical form. We can't change tomorrow until we get there. Deal with that when it's time. For today, choose to be present, breathe deeply, be at peace with yourself and radiate that energy out into the world. Face adversity with compassion and understanding. Not one of us is perfect, but we can aspire to be more than what we were yesterday and inspire others by our actions today.

The practice of living a fully sentient life leads to inner peace, self-mastery, and touches all life forms as we work toward manifesting universal peace.

Treat others as you wish to be treated and may your journey into oneness be for the highest and greatest good of all.

With Love,

Nicole

Additional
Resources

"Paraphysics R&D – Warsaw Pact (U)," DST-1810S-202-78, Defense Intelligence Agency (30 March 1978).

Baron-Cohen, Leslie & Frith, 1988; whereby Baron-Cohen modified a puppet play of Wimmer and Perner (1983).

Boles and Lohmann, 2003; Lohmann, 1996; Lohmann and Lohmann 1994; Light and Salmon, *Magnetic information in animal orientation*; 1993

Christof Koch, Scientific American; May 1, 2015, Intuition May Reveal Where Expertise Resides in the Brain

Gordon PhD, Nancy; *The Guiding Philosophy for the Future of Healthcare*; 2012

H.R. Schiffman, Sensation and Perception, An Integrated Approach, Third Edition, 1976, 1982, 1990, p.452

J. J. Gibson 1966, 1979, 1983, Gibson's Theory of Perceptual Learning.

See also: Gibson p.6, see also Bruce & Green, 1985

Jahn, R.G.; B.J. Dunne (1986), "On the Quantum Mechanics of Consciousness with Application to Anomalous Phenomena," *Foundations of Physics* **18**(6): 721–772

Jeremy Rifkin, The Empathic Civilization, 2009

Joe Lewels, Rulers of the Earth Secret sons of God © 2007; p167, p180-209

Joseph LeDoux, Penguin Books; New York © 2002

Julian Jaynes; *The Origin of Consciousness in the Breakdown of the Bicameral Mind*

Julian Jaynes Scientists Measure Intuition, Live Science

Mark Anderson; February 2009 issue of Discover, Science for the Curious, Is Quantum Mechanics Controlling Your Thoughts?

Mary Bates, WIRED; *Dolphin Hear, Dolphin Do: Imitation by Echolocation;* 3 Oct. 2013; Professor Garth Jones, Science Now, Bats and Dolphins Evolved Echolocation in Same Way, 4 September 2013; A. A. Pack, L.M. Herman & Hoffmann-Kuhnt; *Dolphin echolocation shape perception from sound to object,* The Dolphin Institute, University of Chicago Press; & Sensory integration in the bottle nosed dolphin; Immediate recognition of complex shapes across the senses of echolocation and vision. Journal of Acoustical Society of America, 98, 722-733; & L.M. Herman, A.A. Pack, & M. Hoffman-Kuhnt, (1998) *Seeing through sound: Dolphin perceive the spatial structure of objects through echolocation.*

May 20, 2016, The Science of Intuition, How to Measure Hunches and Gut Feelings by Cari Nierenberg

Microscopic books of DNA as suggested by Werner Loewenstein, The Touchstone of Life, Oxford University Press, Copyright 1999 Werner Loewenstein

Nothing is Solid Everything is Energy, Collective Evolution; September 27, 2014; Arjun Walia

Puthoff, H.E., *"Toward a Quantum Theory of Life Process,"* unpublished proposal, Stanford Research Institute (1972)

Puthoff, Harold E. and Targ, Russell, A Perceptual Channel for Information Transfer over Kilometer Distances: Introduction

Rice University, BC Campus Article, Anatomy Physiology, Chapter 14, 14.1 Sensory Perception

Richard Gerber, *Vibrational Medicine for the 21st Century,* 17; Norm Shealy, *Energy Medicine,* © 1971, 1993-2007

Rifkin, The Empathic Civilization, 2010; Non-fiction, Evolution of Communication and Energy Development

Robert G. Jahn, (1982). The Persistent Paradox of Psychic Phenomena: An Engineering Perspective, Proceedings of the IEEE. Volume 70: 136-170

Robert Titzer; *My Baby Can Read* is a 5 DVD reading system that tutors your baby while it entertains them.

Scientists Measure Communication Between Quantum Entangled Atoms, Stephen Goldmeier;

Mad Science, 06/03/2009

Universe Forum, produced for NASA by Harvard Smithsonian Center for Astrophysics

Dr Michio Kaku, Famed Futurist, Physicist, Bestselling Author, Radio & TV Personality

MIT News, *You can't entangle without a wormhole*, December 5, 2013, Jennifere Chu, MIT News Office

Science, *A Link Between Wormholes and Quantum Entanglement,* 2 December 2013, Katia Moskvitch

Energy.gov Office of Science, *DOE Explains...Quarks and Gluons*

Real Holistic Doc, Dr. Norm Shealy M.D., Ph.D.; see also; Shealy Sorin Wellness Institute, The Original Holistic Health Solution, Shealy Sorin Wellness

Foundation for Alternative and Integrative Medicine, C. Norm Shealy, M.D., Ph.D

The final blank pages have been included for you to journal and note anything that's changed for you since you began reading this material. I have found it particularly useful to note what I have experienced to then go back over my journaling years later.

May your journey have been magical and more fruitful than you could have ever imagined. Be well, be kind, be courageous and love everyone as you would have them love you.

Notes

About the author

Nicole Myers Henderson, best-selling author of I'm So Glad You Left Me: 88 Stories of Courage, Self-Love, and Personal Growth.

Nicole is a speaker/storyteller, a peace advocate, empowerment coach, remote viewer, medical intuitive, owner-operator of SeeInfi nitely.com, and CEO of Grow Well Appalachia, a Nonprofit 501C3 organization located in Northeastern Tennessee where she lives, and loves to work and play in the garden with her husband and loyal canine.

She believes that if humanity is given the proper tools to meet life challenges head-on, together we can create peaceable solutions for the generations to come.

www.ingramcontent.com/pod-product-compliance
Lightning Source LLC
Chambersburg PA
CBHW051133120626
46547CB00012B/779